INSPIRED
MANIFESTING

INSPIRED
MANIFESTING

*Elevate Your Energy &
Ignite Your Dreams
Through the Akashic
Records*

DR. LINDA HOWE

Energy Integrity Publishing

Contents

INTRODUCTION   12

1   An Invitation to a Spiritual Approach   19

2   Ordinary Life Through a Spiritual Lens   29

3   An Introduction to the Akasha   34

4   The Compelling Power of Soul's Purposes   41

5   Assumptions in the Age of Awakening   45

6   How to Read Your Own Akashic Records   53

7   The Soul's Spiritual Nature: A Spiritual Awakening   68

8   Your Soul's Blueprint   80

9   Top 10 Clues You are Living Your Soul's Purpose   89

10   The Magnificent Process of Manifesting   99

11   Manifesting Your Soul's Purposes   109

12   Clearing Obstacles to Manifest Your Destiny   117

13   Robust Manifesting: Money, Prosperity & Abundance   133

14   Supercharging Inspired Manifesting   149

15   Humility, Patience & Peace   158

16   What Does Success Look Like?   171

17 Personal, Perpetual Transformation 175

18 Manifesting our Desires; Seven Steps to Spiritual Success 185

19 Inspired Manifesting & Relationships 193

20 Inspired Manifesting & Your Health 206

21 Inspired Manifesting & Your Spiritual Growth 219

ONWARD! 229

THANK YOU! 233

ABOUT THE AUTHOR 234

ALSO BY DR. LINDA HOWE

How to Read the Akashic Records: Accessing the Archive of the Soul and its Journey (Sounds True 2009)

Healing through the Akashic Records: Using the Power of Your Sacred Wounds to Discover Your Soul's Perfection (Sounds True 2011)

Discover Your Soul's Path through the Akashic Records: Taking Your Life from Ordinary to ExtraOrdinary (Hay House 2015)

Please visit www.LindaHowe.com.

PRAISE FOR INSPIRED MANIFESTING

"*Inspired Manifesting* addresses the challenges that confront all of humanity and provides the reader with a clear understanding of our authentic eternal spiritual self and relationship with the finite physical world of form. It focuses on the spiritual tools necessary for the reader to enhance and empower human life experiences and in the process take dominion over the ever-changing circumstances of the human drama. An enhancing and inspiring read."
—Rev. Dr. Angelo Pizelo, President and Director at Emerson Institute

"*Each of us is on the path of awakening, here to step into our highest potentiality as souls in human form. Thank goodness for master guides like Linda Howe. She shows us exactly how to recall our soul blueprint, receive Divine guidance from the Akasha, and manifest our lives in flow with the Universe. A remarkable and essential guide for living our soul destiny.*"
—Sara Wiseman, Author and Founder of Intuition University

"*In a field crowded with books about attracting and manifesting, Inspired Manifesting is a truly fresh and remarkably empowering approach to what manifesting really is—a set of highly focused and inspirational spiritual technologies to be utilized in combination with a partnership with your own soul and its unique blueprint for you. Readers who apply Dr. Howe's teachings will discover a new way of living and being, which will naturally attract and manifest abundance and activate limitless possibilities. A refreshing, deeply motivating and energetically charged read! Highly recommended!*"
—Karen Stuth, Author, Owner Satiama Publishing & President Coalition of Visionary Resources

"At first glance *Inspired Manifesting* is an expertly guided journey, via every-day life, leading to personal fulfillment, happiness and joy. It's also a genuine trea-sure trove of spiritual truths and teachings that are offered with an ease and grace that belie their life changing possibilities. Linda's writing is so engaging, honest and generous that it creates an ideal environment, like a porous interface, that makes the book itself feel like a living, breathing thing that's capable of a seem-ingly effortless transference of knowledge. Delightful and unassuming, this book is an invitation into a realm of limitless potential. It's a miracle of a book—compas-sionate, inclusive—with enough weight and layers to warrant repeated reading. Ultimately, it left me feeling fortified, empowered, confident and in full possession of the tools needed to begin my own inspired manifesting." —Anne Horrigan, longtime student of the Records

"A long-awaited prescription for manifesting but not a one-size-fits-all. Dr.Howe's wisdom guided me to reveal the dream of my soul through the three-fold connecting principles of heart, mind, and will!" —Dawn Silver DN, As-trologer/Author

"Linda delivers a pragmatic yet pioneering structure by which to connect our spirituality to our lived human experience. Her step-by-step instructions guide us in identifying the promptings of our soul to pursue the pathway that is authenti-cally ours. She makes the art of the possible practical, providing life-long resources that we can draw on during difficult times."
—Patty Collinsworth, Elite Certified Akashic Records Teacher

"*Inspired Manifesting* is a masterful blueprint for welcoming more peace, pros-perity, and possibility into your life. Linda's seven-step process, fueled by the dynamic supportive energy of the Akashic Records, allows you to sidestep the com-mon pitfalls in manifesting, thereby accelerating you toward your soul-inspired dreams. She addresses both the practical and spiritual aspects of manifesting—a potent combination that empowers you as an incarnated soul to positively influ-ence both your world and the world-at-large. What a powerful spiritual resource for these challenging times!" —Christy L. Johnson, Ph.D., Elite Certified Akashic Records Teacher

"The reader will find this book does exactly what the wise Dr. Howe suggests it will: elevate your energy and ignite your dreams—leading to fulfilling relationships, better spiritual practices and strengthened manifestation—all necessary skills in our evolving world." —**Marc St.Camille, Life Coach, Author and Hypnotist**

"Dr. Howe delivers a masterpiece for the ordinary mind to master the journey of the Soul's Purposes. It is truly an exhilarating experience to witness how she extracts simple words to foster such profundity in understanding **Inspired Manifesting**. Her writing style embodies the veritable essence of the Akashic Records; it is so loving, so peaceful, so illumined that one knows that this woman lives from and within the Records. As one reads this expose, one's Soul is soothed and awakened to a wholesome Spiritual Awareness. Dr. Howe's presentation gives us hope through her personal experiences, which explicate her former despair and sense of being lost; yet, now we are privy to her elevation of consciousness. This is the perfect read for anyone who feels stuck and remiss as to "why". It is as if Dr. Howe is saying, 'Enough is Enough! It is high time for those of us who have chosen to be on the planet during this particular time to live to our Soul's Purposes. On your mark, get set, go!'" —**Siri Sat Nam, Ph.D, LMFT**

"At this critical time for humanity, Linda Howe shares a new approach to life: Manifesting in the 21st century is a spiritual venture and we're in a perpetual practice of transformation. This book is full of exercises presented in Linda's down-to-earth and engaging style. Her frequent reminders that all of this can happen in our ordinary human lives makes her work accessible to all those seeking more love and peace in their lives." —**Cathy Kneeland, Owner Circles of Wisdom**

"Using clearly defined terms, step-by-step instructions, and engaging exercises, Linda has written a book of timeless truths perfect for these unsettling times. Best of all, she not only teaches the material, she lives its principles with grace and love. Linda's profoundly simple approach to manifesting through the Records is pure gold for the spiritual sage and student alike. I recommend this book wholeheartedly!"
—**Steffany Barton, RN, Author, Intuitive, Medium**

"Inspired Manifesting offers a new way to review our unique patterning around money. These tools are invaluable to deepen one's soul purpose and enhance co-creation skills for abundant living. I am so grateful for this rich resource, which I will use with clients." —**Rachel Li, MDiv, Certified Professional Coach and Akashic Records Reader**

"Timing is everything and there is no more perfect time than the present to engage in an empowering journey. Inspired Manifesting is a masterfully woven journey for the novice to the most experienced. Linda guides you with delicate, yet direct, support. If you want to find some sense in a year that has challenged every aspect of the human experience, Linda offers the ultimate road map to clarity. These pages are filled with her personal experiences, information, guidance and practical exercises to assist you along the way. This is about empowerment, taking control of your lucid dream." —**Mark A. James, Ph. D., Owner Akashic Awareness**

"Once again Dr. Linda Howe has drawn me in with her wise, inspirational and compassionate offerings. I have been leaning on her teachings for 10+ years. Inspired Manifesting renewed my desire to become even more aligned with my Soul's Purposes and to fully inhabit this human experience. I recommend this book to everyone waking up to their potential, looking for a spark to ignite their inner flame, or needing practices that will move them into action." —**Kirsten Harwick, longtime student of the Records, SilentSynergy.com**

"This book upends what we learned about The Law of Attraction. What a relief to know that there's an easier way! Linda Howe provides multiple avenues to explore how to manifest in any area of our life, with loving care at the root of each sojourn. Inspired Manifesting will move you to tears, instill hope, and provide practical ways to explore your way to a richer, more fulfilled you. Gain greater understanding to attract more love in your life and reflect that back to others." —**Maria K. Benning, Certified Akashic Records Teacher**

Dedicated to All Seekers and Finders of the Light

Rejoice in the way things are.
When you realize there is nothing lacking,
the whole world belongs to you.

Tao te Ching, by Stephen Mitchell
(Translation 1988 Harper Perennial #44)

....

November 2020

My Dear Reader,

I always teach what I am learning. The same is true for this manifesting project. This book is a reporting of my own journey and growth as I learned to manifest my own soul's purposes in the world in which I find myself. When I started this book, I was certain I'd follow a traditional path of publishing. But then the pandemic hit with a vengeance. Along with it came changes I never anticipated. Some I actually swore I'd never do. Well, one of the many silver linings in the Covid-19 cloud was my experience of setting aside my prejudices and experimenting with new ways of engaging in the world. Then I found myself in a serious crunch: Wondering how to get this valuable book into circulation ASAP—or not...taking a slow, route and missing a once-in-many-lifetimes opportunities?

So, here I am, self-publishing and here you are, open to receiving important guidance about how to live your dreams in times of epic change and finding Inspired Manifestation at this perfect moment in time. The power nugget woven through this book is this: The essence of your heartfelt desires is precisely what our changing world is missing. You—being you, doing you—are what the world needs now. Let go of the way it "should" be, surrender your demands and offer your service in the most efficient, effective way available at this moment. Life is waiting for each of us to step up and join the fun.

Let's go! Onward!

Love, *Linda*

INTRODUCTION

Welcome!

We are living in times of dramatic change. But you, my friend, already know this simple fact. You are among the many involved in their own awakening, stimulated by sophisticated communications linking us to one another, alerting us to instantaneous shifts in the ground we once assumed was solid. This is both exciting and challenging for everyone—whether we are fully alert and enthusiastic, feeling startled into awakening against our better judgment, or slowly and deliberately shedding the vestiges of our old self, waiting for the latest version to come into focus.

"Why did we choose to be here, now?" we chuckle to ourselves, as we question our intentions to be here on earth at this very precise time in history. Our enhanced sensitivity alerts us to the immense possibilities of our time. Why we chose to be on the planet during this time of epic change raises many questions, as we live through the process. As visionaries inspired by the ultimate completion of change, we may overlook the path to transformation, which naturally includes the dissolution of old ideas and institutions, and the demolition of obstructions to our envisioned results.

Newly alert to the potential of our dreams, we may minimize the tenacity of our accepted values, and experience fierce resistance to opportunities for growth and change. Personally, I prefer to skip the turmoil of the transition, the collision of traditions and contemporary ideas, and keep my attention firmly resting on my preferred final outcome. Although this is a great strategy in many cases, the changes occurring here on earth, through everyday human beings, within ordinary time, can be messy.

Yet these are the opportunities of our time. All of us have chosen to be here for this exceptional—albeit uncomfortable—passage in human evolution. And this understanding raises the $50 million question, "What were we thinking?"

I understand this confusion. How is it possible that we are living in times of unprecedented possibilities, unlimited options, wide ranges of choices—and yet, at the very same time, we frequently feel foggy, uncertain, frightened, and sometimes even on the edges of despair?

My Personal Quest

Since my life-changing moment of spiritual awareness at the age of 24, my focus, attention and energy have been dedicated to enhancing my consciousness to discover and include a spiritual perspective. "How do I know God while here on earth?" has been the primary question propelling my journey. And this has led to my exploring religions of every sort, as well as self-help programs and exoteric/esoteric programs for igniting spiritual awareness.

By the age of 40, having plumbed the depth of countless avenues, I found myself catapulted into the heart of the Akashic Records, which I have come to know as my spiritual home. Embraced by this infinite spiritual dimension, I've been graced with willingness, curiosity and tenacity, enough to mine its riches. As a result, I've created a series of movement-inspiring, award-winning books, a comprehensive curriculum for personal growth and transformation, and earned the distinction of being the first person on the planet to design and be awarded a Doctorate in Spiritual Studies with a concentration in the Akashic Records for personal growth and transformation. All of this work has advanced my own personal growth, while empowering students and inspired seekers on every continent. What a privilege and honor it has all been!

My decades of deliberate attention to spiritual light and truth helped me recognize that this time of turbulence is neither punishment nor indictment of human unworthiness. Rather, this time is for our awakening awareness of truth— mine and yours. The magnitude of this challenge cannot be underestimated.

Challenging Times Mandate New Solutions

Compounding the difficulty is the fact that all of our tried and true strategies for successful engagement in the world in honorable, productive ways are falling apart. They are not working at a time when we need solutions more than ever. After centuries of trying to resolve planetary issues—ranging from political, economic, social, cultural, environmental and all the rest—by working on the results, the effects, the facts as we identify them in the world, we have come to know the limitations of this approach. While it's possible to re-route our difficulties and temporarily resolve big external matters, until the inner causes are addressed, and conditions supporting true growth encouraged, we'll always return to our old ways.

In order to move in a different direction, our new path must be much more inviting than the old one. It must touch our hearts, inspire our thoughts, and invigorate us to act. If it is not measurably more appealing than our tried and true ways, we won't do it. What is that special something that will resurrect us from our old ideas and patterns, and move us into an unknown but trustworthy new path?

First, we need new questions to guide our discovery process. It will take courage to entertain new points of view, and generate sufficient willingness to experiment with the unknown.

The possibility that this personal and collective transformation is for our benefit is downright radical and exciting. If I can consider all these seemingly unrelated elements of life—the chaos and confusion—as the next stage of expanding goodness for me personally, well, that's a great idea. But, unfortunately, I don't know many who are viewing these times through such a lens. What we need instead is a viewfinder constructed with unconditionally loving, accepting, honorable elements. One that provides a portal through which we can examine and explore these significant aspects of our changing life, one that is loving, judgment-free, and fearless. From this perspective, there's nothing to resist. A point of view that is unafraid of the ugly, nasty expressions of life brought by fearful humans is indeed a worthy project. We also need a new perspective for observing and evaluating our experiences. A point of view clear in intent could support and empower us to discover for ourselves practical, approaches to inspire our everyday living. This is the time for us to adapt a lens that empowers us to identify the presence of light and love even in the face of absolutely zero evidence. And that lens must be spiritual, to illuminate the living energy of love.

The New View Must Be Spiritual

A spiritual point of view is especially effective because it provides an infinite context, an eternally expanding framework for visible and invisible perspectives. It is both familiar and yet-to-be-discovered, while also respectful of time, space and human reality. What's more, all other perspectives—from scientific to emotional and everything in-between—are naturally included in the spiritual point of view. They can, in fact, be recognized as particular expressions of a fundamental spiritual context, which serves as the foundation for all other points of view.

While other perspectives have their place and benefits, we need a comprehensive, loving, spiritual approach to the conundrums of 21st century life. We are desperate for an approach that makes it easier for us to be authentic and vulnerable, as well as emotionally safe, so we have permission to be honest. In that process, we can discover new paths for empowering awareness, acceptance and appropriate action so that we can begin living lives which represent our greatest truths and highest aspirations.

Once we adopt a spiritual perspective, we can consider what we seek to transform our relationship with this ordinary life. I know that somewhere deep within my being, there is a dimension encoded with my ultimate potential, a sliver of divine consciousness, which expresses and radiates infinite love through me into life. This is my Soul, the part of me that is Divine in nature, which embodies the whole of Universal goodness and life. This fragment of the Universal whole links me to all other humans, as well as to the entirety of creation.

I want to know this aspect of my being, its nature and purposes. I long for this awareness of Soul and its purposes. This is the amazing opportunity of our time, and each of us is here to consciously recognize our Soul's Purposes and express them—while being mere mortals. How easy it will be, once I am free of this body, to enjoy all the blessings of Soul. But, while I am still human, the challenge is significant.

Now is the Time

Now is an ideal time to initiate the new—to begin to view life and all its wonders from a spiritual perspective, to examine the innermost reaches of the self—the Soul—to learn what it is and how to be in a more conscious relationship with this dimension of our being. And yes, to identify and bring Soul's Purposes to life!

With this platform in place, we can consider Inspired Manifesting. Discovering the remarkable opportunity of consciously manifesting our Soul's Purposes opens the way to a future many of us consider to be a dream. More than that, these treasures of inner awareness are the seeds of the new Heaven on earth. Together, we can engage in a transformational process and bring the riches of our hearts to the world—to experience, express and enjoy them right here, right now.

Are You Ready?

Consider whether any of these questions resonate with you:

No matter how much you've already accomplished in this life, do you have a feeling that so much more is possible?

Are you ready to take your next steps to discover what's possible for you, and how to live in the realm of realizing your potential?

Do you now have a sense that deep within you is a treasury of unidentified gifts, under-developed talents and minimized abilities that you would gladly share if only you could grasp them?

Do pesky blockages keep surfacing almost every time you're ready to venture forth to make your dreams come true?

Have you noticed undesirable patterns of behavior that worm their way through your best efforts and compound your challenges, undermining your hard-earned progress?

Have you tried so many ways to ignore, eliminate and overcome these obstacles and patterns, with less than permanent success?

If so, now is your time, and this is the lifetime for you to awaken to a new perspective, empowering you to extend only love to yourself and others. This is available when you view yourself through the unconditionally loving lens of your Soul. After that, nothing will ever be the same again!

This Book's Purpose

The purpose of this book is to empower you to grow in awareness to expand your self-acceptance, experience and express your Soul's Purposes, so that you can appreciate your earthly life for what it is. Your empowerment in these areas will propel you into a new dimension of inner peace and joy. Your visions of fulfilling possibilities are clues to your Soul's intentions biding their time until you are ready, willing and able to make them tangible here on earth. To increase your conscious awareness of your Soul's Purposes, first you need to find ways to be an emotionally safe, supportive listener, so you can plumb the depths of honesty about yourself, as well as your motives and desires. This initiates the process of greater inner peace and acceptance, which naturally accelerates the dissolution of obstructions, confusions and limitations. Your personal embrace of freedom ignites your awakening awareness so you can discover fulfilling ways to express your deepest truths. As you bring the best of yourself to life, you activate the unlimited love living inside, and encounter the joy of living, inspiring yourself and others to your next level of possibility.

This is a time like no other. In ages past, we had either an awareness of greater truths, or phases of opportunity or even recognized the needs of our world, but now, we stand at the precipice of this trifecta (awareness + opportunity + needs), empowered by who we are as people.

We are optimal instruments for the realization of our Soul's Purposes, at an exceptional moment in human evolution. Our awesome opportunity as awakening individuals is to recognize our Destiny, discover our Soul's Intentions and bring our Soul's Purposes to life. This is the lifetime for freely manifesting our unique contributions, consciously, responsibly and deliberately, with unbridled aliveness and ultimate fulfillment. This is our time. Join me, your traveling companion on the great spiritual pathway of life.

One of the most pleasurable ventures here on earth is pursuing spiritual truths for growth and transformation, together. We know there are some parts of the quest we must do alone, some segments of the transformational way require us to take solo. There are other times, however, that are meant to be shared, and this is one such passage. None of us is equipped to single-handedly navigate life—that's why there are so many of us on earth at any given time. Additionally, sharing the adventure makes it more inspiring and way more enjoyable. It is, in fact, critical that we find suitable traveling companions, that we connect with others for assistance and uplift. A spiritual journey requires focused attention, willingness, honest reflection, patience, and practice. Even more important is a sincere desire to become more than you ever thought possible. The very fact that my words found you is evidence that you're ready. Our generous Universe cosmically nudged you to step onto this spiritual pathway.

Now is the ideal time to begin, and you are the perfect person. So, let's get started. Imagine that you and I are sitting together at my kitchen table, as I reach out my hand to you. Here we go!

I

An Invitation to a Spiritual Approach

One of our first tasks is to clarify the terms we'll be using, beginning with the word spiritual. This word is tossed about with casual abandon and, in some circles, seems to include magical processes and supernatural abilities. For our purposes, though, let's open our minds to the truth of being rooted in spirit—the primary feature of spirit is love. Other qualities come into focus as well, such as peace, light, harmony and aliveness, among others. When using the word spiritual (or its derivatives: spirit, inspired, inspirational), I'm referring to the aspect that is unconditionally loving. The essence of love is the heart of an inspired or spiritual approach. So, when speaking of being spiritual, I'm referring to loving.

Based on this definition, it becomes easier to recognize what is truly spiritual. The test is this: "Is this loving?" If it's loving, it's spiritual, and I feel inspired. If not, it's something other than spiritual.

Manifesting is another term deserving clarification. To manifest is to demonstrate, to make something that's invisible become visible, to give form to an idea. You may have noticed a surge in popularity of this word recently—I certainly have. Manifesting calls for clear thinking to understand what it's all about. It's about bringing our inner hopes and dreams into the recognized reality of our human lives. And, while humans are always manifesting, our intention is to learn how to use this ability to manifest more of what we want, and less of what we don't want. Let's look a bit deeper.

Here in the West, the consumer culture introduced in the 1950s, which was in full swing by the 1980s, told us what manifesting should look like—and it was all about prosperity and financial abundance. You may recall some of the common themes of those decades, such as "the material world matters most" and "plastic is king." We did our best to exert our will and increase our efforts to achieve those measures of success, believing that this was the highest form of manifesting. We expected life to respond in predictable and measurable ways. The only problem was that life did not respond as expected—and eventually, we began to realize that perhaps this was not Inspired Manifesting.

What is Inspired Manifesting?

Some view human beings as completely dependent upon cultural and socio- economic forces beyond their control. They think that we're engaged in an epic battle, fighting external forces. Some of us believed that the next generation would exceed their parents' success, while others were too afraid to risk going beyond the limits imposed by familial and cultural structures. Still others believe that we're here merely to survive, biding our time until we escape to an otherworldly paradise. Many of these worldviews are alive and well on our planet today—keeping us separated and stuck in survival mode. Can you see that these, too, are not Inspired Manifesting?

We've been stuck between two primary interpretations of manifestation: One, that in order to bring our deepest desires to our lives, we have to marshal the forces of our will, and force our way into demonstration, and two, being victimized as we are makes the treasures of our innermost being so remote that it's best to forget them. Neither of these options is complete, much less helpful. We must look beyond them to resolve our confusion.

Spiritual confusion—our individual and collective discontent and dissatisfaction—has taken a large toll on humanity. Not experiencing our unique usefulness has left us feeling isolated, depressed and anxious. How tragic that some of us are quite convinced that things are hopeless, especially because there are so many reasons to feel hopeful. Engaging fully with this new approach to Inspired Manifesting will alleviate suffering, confusion and loneliness. This new perspective makes it easier to move into life and participate, rather than escaping to the nearest mountain top.

There is a realm of infinite possibilities, where our heartfelt human desires intersect with planetary life, where our dreams combine with life in surprisingly predictable ways. This doesn't mean we can force our preferred outcomes. But we can count on the consistency of this realm. As we let go of our hopes into this space of engagement, they connect and blend with life, what we know about life, as well as the hidden potentials of life. Amazing things happen. Have you ever released your hopes to the Universe and discovered something even better happened than what you'd hoped? This is the realm of infinite possibilities, where we let go so this alchemical process can take its course. Voila!—Manifestation.

Here I offer you a brand new paradigm. I propose a new way of living in the world and describe how you can start today: as you are, right here, right now, with what you have. I am championing an entire transformation of your relationship with life so that you can enjoy exceptional, extraordinary relationships. I want to empower you to live in the sweet spot where your perfectly Divine essence meets your imperfect humanity. I believe it is possible for us to enjoy heaven on earth—to encounter, experience and express our Divine light and unconditional love through our ordinary human selves. THIS is Inspired Manifesting.

Manifestation is a spiritual process based on spiritual principles that generates physical evidence of this magnificent spiritual reality: We are unconditional love in person, and our nature is interconnectedness. The remarkable result is enjoying the blessing of living our Destiny. While not easy, this simple process is the fast track to living a life rich with meaning and engagement, where every human encounter expresses Divine light and love, right here on earth. This perspective illuminates the realities that we are one woven together by threads of connection, and that we are here to express and experience unconditional love.

A Bit More About Me

Like you, I did not always experience the reality of oneness. Truthfully, I felt like an outsider for much of my life, even in my own family. Growing up, we were one of a few Catholic families in the neighborhood. Among many, many cousins, I was the only lesbian, the only one to adopt children and the only mother of a black child. So of course, I saw plenty of reasons to feel alone, different, isolated. Seeking acceptance from others made me feel worse.

After discovering the spiritual resource of the Akashic Records and working in my own Records to consciously recognize my Soul's Purposes, I learned that I am here to experience unity (especially when it appears that there is none) and to realize interconnectedness (even in the face of feeling separation). As it turns out, my wound (feeling like an outsider) was actually a portal for discovering the truth of my Soul. Once I embraced my uniqueness and learned to unconditionally love and accept myself, I experienced an expanded sense of connection.

My primary Soul's Purpose (as is yours) is experiencing unconditional love and expressing this love to others. In doing so, we have an opportunity to develop our gifts, talents, skills, and abilities and to relinquish our immaturities, weaknesses and fears. Some ways I express my Soul's Purposes are through teaching and writing. In order to manifest my Soul's Purposes, I must constantly practice setting aside judgment, fears and perfectionism. As I do so, I experience great happiness, joy and satisfaction. Being involved and engaged in manifesting my Soul's Purposes ignites the unconditional love within me.

At the beginning of my journey, the secret desire of my heart was to find away to consciously relate to myself, to others and to life, which put me in direct contact with the Source. In spite of my endless imperfections, this is precisely what has become the most ordinary, albeit extraordinary, feature of my life. I have lived my way into experiencing a family, a career, the Linda Howe Center for Akashic Studies, and written multiple books that have been translated into multiple languages and sold around the world. I've also delivered my teaching through online platforms that didn't exist when I took the first steps. In the past few years, I began traveling to Asia to teach thousands of eager students wanting to enjoy a more conscious connection with their own soul, and activate their understanding and expression of their Soul's Purposes. My journey manifesting my Soul's Purposes has exceeded my wildest imaginings. It has been far more fulfilling than I ever anticipated. And yet, this has all happened quite naturally, by me responding to my very ordinary life.

Within every one of us, there's a knowing that this is the time to awaken, to upgrade our lives, to answer the call, to bring the precious richness of our Souls into the world. For decades, this inner awareness has been a persistent longing of mine, and I've noticed, of every student I've ever taught and every seeker I've met along the way. As a child, I thought spiritual awakening was a special opportunity reserved only for certain individuals. Yet, as time has carried us into the 21st century, this sacred opportunity has become available to everyone—opening up a treasure trove of wonderful options not yet fully realized.

When I initially stood at the threshold of this remarkable potential, I felt confused about the nature of the Soul. Befuddled, I questioned the necessity of expressing my Soul's Purposes. How could this be valuable? Talk in New Age circles about manifestation made me wonder what would be required. Brain fog enveloped me like a multilayered cloud. But diving into my own personal exploration, followed by experimentations with my students and an examination of the collective consciousness, I compiled quite a stack of papers—all of my insights scribbled down—which are now organized here and shared with you.

The link between spirituality and manifesting has been exploited in books, on radio shows, summits, and podcasts—so many of us clamoring for a golden kernel of simple truth that brings peace of mind, and material reward. What's the motivation behind this momentous storm front driving the idea of manifestation into the open? This time in the evolution of human consciousness has brought the dawning of awareness of human and divine will, based on a heart and mind partnership that has allowed many of us to realize greater harmony between our inner truth and the outer world. While this realization has come at the perfect time, many of us still sense that something is missing. As essential as the foundational heart/mind connection is, it is also incomplete.

Those of us who have toiled valiantly to perfect this partnership—but have still fallen short of making our dreams come true in everyday life—need not persecute ourselves anymore. As a human being intent on living a full experience, there is always more to understand. Surveying my students, I realized this beautiful truth: None of us are spiritual slackers nor do we suffer an ancient ancestral curse. In fact, we are all human beings, currently alive on the planet to participate in the birth of a new dimension of awareness—one that will catapult us into the fullness of our humanity, increase a more conscious connection with the Divine, and ultimately manifest our Soul's Purposes here on earth.

With the revelation of this insight, the next segment of my journey became increasingly clear, and far less daunting. Recognizing the limitations of a heart/mind approach, I began to see the possibilities of a three-dimensional framework (heart + mind + will). Hopeful, my growing enthusiasm brought new questions:

What is will?

How does it operate?

How do I cultivate my personal relationship with it?

What is the Soul?

What are my Soul's Purposes?

What is destiny all about?

What is co-creation?

What about personal responsibility?

What is the connection between my Soul and the human being I am in this lifetime?

How can I remain fully awake to the spiritual truth of my personal identity and treat my community with love and respect?

I realized the futility of straining to think my way into spiritual satisfaction or to feel into the way of enlightenment. While mind and heart are absolute essentials, alone they are not enough. It is time to open up to the next dimension of awareness—our will. Deliberately aligning our will with mind and heart, we become consciously multi-dimensional beings! We have always been multi-dimensional creatures, but now the exquisite opportunity for us to be awake and aware of this feature of our being. Our will is located in that place where our Soul's Purposes meet planetary life, creating the requisite force for action and tangible results here on earth. The will is the point of power, through which soul impulses take form in the world. It is a place in consciousness, not a literal location, so don't strain to find it. Just savor the idea—it's downright liberating.

And yet, some Law of Attraction stories have left seekers wondering why we can't attract everything we want. Rest assured, if you can't cheer, meditate or hypnotize yourself into who you want to be, you are in good company. While the awareness of our will is growing, we still don't know what to do with it. Those on the front lines know there is more to come. The leap required for will to be woven into mass consciousness is tremendous.

We are the first generation in human history with this stunning awareness and privilege of making conscious choices steering our own process. There are no role models for this experiment. As the front runners in this evolutionary exercise, we are invited to experiment and evaluate for ourselves and make decisions based on our assessments. I appreciate that, since we are the first, perfection is not required. Ample room exists for us to intuit, act and access. To learn by discovering what works for us and what doesn't, without the pressure of prior standards. How lucky to have this opportunity! It's truly exciting and also, a bit frightening.

Why a Spiritual Approach?

Consider that your essence is love, as is the core of every other person on the planet. Imagine seeing yourself and others through the lens of unconditional love. Unconditional is a powerful word, implying "no matter what." Can you possibly perceive yourself as loving and lovable in all situations? Is there any chance you can extend this same point of view to others—those you understand, and those you don't? This is an example of a truly spiritual approach, adapting a viewfinder that locates only love and light, peace and goodness. One that refuses to register anything called evil or bad. To be sure this is an outrageous point of view, and also, nothing short of life changing. Within each of us lies the raw material for cultivating this perspective. Helping us to identify ourselves and others as we are seen and known through the eyes of the Divine. Our opportunity is to allow ourselves to grow into it.

This spiritual approach is both simple and transformational. Thousands of my students around the world are now living more loving lives—expressing their inspired Soul's Purposes—than ever before, all as a result of learning this process and Inspired Manifesting. This is a wildly exciting idea, I know, so let's pause now to get centered before you learn this inspired approach.

Pause to Reflect

We will start with a simple meditation, and then add more skills as awareness expands. With each of these reflections and meditation practices throughout, I suggest you clear time and space before attempting. Make sure any possible distractions are turned off. I also highly recommend that you have a journal and pen available to record your findings.

A Centering Meditation

Begin by opening your awareness—mind, body and soul—and directing your attention to your physical presence on our planet, right here, right now. You are a human being standing in a particular location, living in a precise time, walking through the world on a specific day. Placing all of your attention on yourself, you may notice that you occupy a particular place, a space in time that you share with no one else. You are the unique spiritual being residing in your human body. Life created this place just for you.

There is not now, nor has there ever been, nor will there ever be, another person just like you. I invite you to stand in this beautiful, powerful truth. You are a unique individual who has come to this place and time as the perfect person to bring your Soul's Purposes to life. No matter what fears or limiting beliefs you hold, you are the ideal person for manifesting your Soul's Purposes. Take your rightful place. Let yourself fully occupy this place and moment in time. And as you do, the light of life is the core of your being, proudly shines itself through you, as you, out into your world.

As you proceed with this work, know this truth: You Are Here to Bring Your Soul's Purposes to Life! You came to succeed in this magnificent mission. And, this may come as a surprise to you, but you can do so in your very ordinary daily life. Let me show you how, beginning with a remarkable story from my own unremarkable life.

2

Ordinary Life Through a Spiritual Lens

A recent experience—viewed through this spiritual lens—had an incredible impact on me. You have certainly had similar events in your life, and so I invite you to recall your own moments of profound spiritual awareness as I share my story with you. Interestingly, as I finalize this manuscript, we are in "Shelter in Place" mode in the United States, protecting ourselves from the coronavirus (AKA Covid-19), which means I am currently prohibited from traveling anywhere, much less to China.

My Extraordinary Story, on a Day in China of All Places:

Since I was first invited to teach others how to access the Akashic Records in China five years ago, I have been traveling to Shanghai to teach hundreds of students several times a year. While each multi-week trip is an adventure worthy of its own telling, my most recent adventure presents an ideal illustration of the process of Manifesting.

As was our usual custom, my host picked me up at the airport.

I have become familiar enough with the landscape to notice that he was taking a far longer route than usual. As it turns out, he had chosen a new location for our class but had failed to tell my business manager. My need to trust life as it is began at that moment. Since this would be my biggest class ever (340 students!), I knew I needed to conserve every ounce of my energy. There was no sense losing it over a minor location change, despite the additional time added to our drive.

I settled into the new hotel, and surrendered to the expanded class size and all the supporting logistics required to accommodate more students. Teaching two different levels of students five days at a time, I had only one full day off in between. On the morning of day three of the first session, the host approached me while I was teaching to let me know that, "Someday you may have to talk to the authorities." I continued teaching until "someday" became right now.

I was escorted to the ground floor of the hotel, into an eating room, and left alone with an interpreter and five 30-year-old Chinese men ("the authorities") who resembled the baddest-ass guys I'd ever seen in any movie. I couldn't tell if they spent more time at the gym or in the bars, but I could see that they were humorless and armed with plenty of cigarettes and large electronic devices. As I was wondering whether the interpreter was sharing all the questions and comments, they demanded my papers and spent a good, long time studying, discussing and circulating them.

Odd as it sounds, I remember noticing the fruit bowl in the center of the table and how delicate the teacups looked in these guys' large, life-worn hands. My first thought—"What am I going to do with my students?" soon became, "What if they take me to jail?" I could sense I was on the verge of really losing it. Maybe my business manager and spouse had been right after all, and this was a bridge too far for a nearly 70-year-old woman to be traveling solo, thousands of miles away from home.

But here I was, in this room together, at this moment in time, each of us just doing our best. Each with our own personal sense of self coupled with our own individual perception of life, and our relationship to it. Wondrously, my awareness shifted to "What is the worst possible thing that can happen to me?" With that, an overwhelming sense of peace came over me, along with this essential truth: "Even if I go to prison, I'll be okay. Sure, it will be terrible and uncomfortable, and I may never see my family again ... but I will be fine."

I smiled politely, made "small talk," and responded as needed while the interrogation continued for nearly an hour. I got it: this was not personal. These men had a job to do, and they were doing it. In that magical moment of grace, I had a sense that my relationship with life itself is far beyond my limited human understanding. So, I respectfully cooperated with the authorities until they finally released me.

After an hour of serious discernment and dialogue (of which I understood very little), they informed me through my interpreter that I didn't have the right visa. They ordered me not to return without proper papers, then they disappeared as mysteriously as they had arrived. I returned to my classroom and resumed teaching as if nothing had happened. I won't forget my interpreter's comment after it was all over. "Oh, Linda, this is how governments are," she said. I emphatically disagreed, "No," I told her. "All governments definitely do not act this way."

I must admit that, after that intense afternoon, I had a sense that the rest of my trip would go smoothly. I survived THIS, so I deserve a pass. However, life treated me to yet another stormy experience. A typhoon slammed into Shanghai. Chinese protections ensued so I could continue teaching (read: towels and buckets). As unpleasant and difficult as this experience was from the moment I landed in Shanghai, I felt completely aligned with life, and in the flow of my Soul's Purposes. Manifesting my Soul's Purposes felt like my only option.

As a matter of fact, this experience turned out to be the highest, clearest and very best laboratory for understanding my relationship to life. No matter what, I know I can love and respect myself, and experience and express this unconditional love to others. It is quite clear that my willingness to risk participating in this messy, chaotic, stormy dance of life—despite my uncomfortable state of not know-ing—is precisely why this was such a meaningful, useful experience. I believe that all of us, from the hundreds of students to the interpreter to the interrogators to me, were called by the blueprint of our Souls to show up in this experience.

The scene was set to accelerate our awakening, so long as we noticed the opportunity: a sliver of life, stark on the edges, a bolt of lighting through the sky to illuminate some simple facts. Life is good. Every event is an opportunity to connect more consciously with the infinite love present in each person, and between us all. Every circum-stance is designed for us to know and love ourselves greater than be-fore, and to register the truth that life loves us all unconditionally. On one hand, it's all exquisitely personal and, on another, it's totally im-personal. There is a convergence of paradox, and our awareness of the paradox becomes the platform for a spiritual leap.

Trusting that I am a precise fit for the needs of the world at this time empowers me to navigate adventures like this. It feels as though my personal Soul and life choose to partner at this particular time, and in this specific way. Each is an opportunity for me to dis-cover more about myself—even though I didn't really comprehend this lesson until a week later at the Iowa State Fair, while watching the sheep judging contest and gnawing on a pork-chop-on-a-stick.

I offer this story to you as a terrific example of Inspired Man-ifestation. While I had absolutely no control or authority over any of the events in China, I had the potent power of awareness of my Soul's Purposes in relationship to the entire creation. I was aware of my own good faith, as well as the highest ideals of all the participants. None of us were looking to harm one another, only to sort through some ques-tions and do our jobs. Increasing my awareness that life is good, there was no reason to be afraid.

By trusting that I am living from the deepest desires of my heart—desires that stimulate my experience of unconditional love in any and all situations—I have more energy to show up, to let go and know what is mine to do. I become increasingly aware of the impulses of my Soul to experience and express love. In this instance, all I could do was to be myself, to respect and engage with the authorities, and then to teach my students. Rather than ramping up my anxiety and fear, I dialed down my resistance, accepted the circumstances, and experienced the calm that comes from dancing with the flow of life. This was nothing short of miraculous for me (my usual tendency is to refuse to accept life in uncomfortable moments). In that mysterious realm, I discovered that I was safe, that I had what I needed and, even more, I experienced knowing that I am part of all of life.

Arriving home, I noticed more clarity about who I am and what is mine to do. My perspective shifted. I felt less fearful than before the trip. Things that triggered me before have little effect on me now. I feel more joyful, and more capable of experiencing pleasure, especially from life's smallest treasures. I often catch myself wondering, Why am I so happy? Because bringing our Soul's Purposes to life, feeling like I am an essential part of the wholeness of life, is so joyful!

Trust me—if it can happen for me, then it certainly can for you, too.

3

An Introduction to the
Akasha

Some of my greatest spiritual allies along the path are the Akashic Records. Several decades ago, when I discovered the Pathway Prayer to Access the Heart of the Akashic Records©, I learned that the power of the Akasha lies in letting the light of life illuminate our own wisdom.

In this chapter, I'll introduce my Pathway Prayer Process© approach so you can learn to trust yourself in accessing your inner wisdom. This is not a full study of the Akashic Records (please see my other books for that). Of course, you are free to use whatever method you like to access a spiritual approach. But let's begin with the one that's been most proven for me, the Akashic Records.

Nature of the Akashic Realm

The Akashic Records can be understood as the energetic connective tissue between the Soul (both universal and individual) and the Source. The Akashic Realm is also the intersecting zone of heaven and earth, the realm where both meet and interface, overlap and harmonize. At the level of the individual, this is where each person connects with life. We come to life with our destiny encoded in our Akashic Records, woven into the fabric of our Soul. The natural heat released by the friction between potential and raw materials unleashes who we are, and manifestation begins.

As the intersection zone of Heaven and earth, the Records are ideal for exploring our personal Soul's Purposes. This is the arena for us to become aware of our inner truth. As we take action, we see what is real or unreal, feasible or impossible, and we adjust. We observe and evaluate how the world receives and responds to what we offer and, again, we make more adjustments. This is how the work of manifestation begins. At a deeper level, we are talking about spiritual healing in action. All of life is spiritual light and love, expressing itself in physical form, here on earth. This is the true nature of the earthly experience.

Importantly, our transformation occurs "through" the Akashic Records, rather than "by" the Records. Conscious awareness of the Akasha supports our growth; the Akasha does not cause growth. The Akashic atmosphere is non-intrusive and non-invasive, allowing us to examine and explore the wisdom infused in the fabric of our Souls, which has been cultivated throughout our lifetimes. In the Akashic Realm, emotional neutrality born of infinite compassion and understanding provides an exceptionally open environment. Without emotional demand or pressure, the light of truth shines freely, and is more easily recognized. Within this realm, we have the opportunity to identify choices and recognize corresponding actions providing options in our lives.

When working within the Akashic Realm, we enter into an even more deliberate, intentional, co-creative partnership with the Divine. As the Akashic field is respectful of our human potential, this infinite spiritual resource is ideal for stimulating a more conscious connection with our Soul. An Akashic atmosphere facilitates inspiration of awareness, acceptance, and appreciation of our humanness, fostering our ability to experience and express love. Engaging with the

Akashic Records, as with any genuine spiritual resource, empowers us to recognize the loving essence of every being. As pure intentions become increasingly real, our interpretations shift, our fears and resentments collapse in the light of truth and love. One of the ways we can be certain we are employing this approach appropriately is when we see the loving truth even when behaviors are messy.

From an Akashic Perspective, everyone is essentially good. There are no "bad" people. All people, no matter how heinous their behavior, are infinitely loving at the center of their being. Through an Akashic lens, we recognize humans as loving beings whose primary drive is to enhance their own experience of love, sense of safety, belonging and value in the world and, of course, peace of mind. This does not rationalize or justify the terrible behavior. It seeks only to gain clarity about the governing principle underneath the behavior. Through the Akashic lens, the Soul is perfect, whole and complete.

There are many subtleties to having an active practice of working in your Records. If you are eager to learn more, or to learn how to read the Records of others, you can read my book How to Read the Akashic Records. But let me tell you one more very important tidbit. When you open the Records using the Pathway Prayer Process © to Access the Heart of the Records, you will be fully conscious and you will be the boss. No uninvited wisps of psychic dust will come to you, no frightening images or mean-spirited phantoms will haunt you.

For centuries, we mere mortals have been victims of our spiritual ideas, scaring ourselves and our loved ones silly with fear-based interpretations of unfamiliar phenomena. Lucky for us, those days are long gone. We no longer have to be victims of our spiritual connections. No more unwelcome hauntings, creepy whispers in the dark, curses or spells thwarting our progress. Each one of us is the boss of our inner life, with the authority and permission to advocate and intervene on our own behalf when necessary. If some unseen creature is bothering you, send them away. You are the boss! And, if it seems like any of these pesky rascals pay you a visit, tell them to leave you alone. If they refuse, tell them I said so!

Hierarchy and Organization of the Akasha

In the Prayer, we refer to the "Lords of the Records" and the "Masters, Teachers and Loved Ones." But who are they? Let me introduce them to you:

Lords of the Akashic Records are Beings of light who have never incarnated. We do not see them, or interact with them directly. They work together as a group, without need for personal gratification. They focus solely on maintaining the integrity of the Akashic Records. Their job is to take care of the Records.

Masters are also Beings of light who never incarnate. They have been with us for all of time, since the inception of our Soul, guiding our awakening through our human journey. Their job is to make sure we wake up. They function as a group orchestrating our unfolding, and need no personal attention from us to do so.

Teachers are Beings of light who may or may not have been in body at some point in time. They are theme- or lesson-specific specialists who stay with us until we embody their particular teaching (such as patience, self-respect, self-trust, etc.). Once realized, they move on to another Soul. Unlike angels or spirit guides, they work cooperatively with other Teachers, without revealing their personal identities.

Loved Ones are those we have known in this lifetime who are now deceased. They are committed to our expanding awareness of our own Souls, and the truth of our essence. They assist us from the other side with comfort, encouragement, and guidance.

Masters, Teachers and Loved Ones work together in groups with no need for personal attention. Our readings are not about them, but about and for us. What distinguishes these of light from others, like spirit guides or angels who are not present or active within the Akashic Field, is that they never assume individual identities for us to recognize. They are so advanced that they are quite comfortable with relinquishing all ego needs and dedicate themselves to our service. Never do they impose themselves on us, not even for a friendly visit. This is not the nature of this serious but loving group of light Beings. Our growth and consciousness development is of utmost importance to them.

There's never any need to pray to them. They are not deities, nor are they errant beings for our dreams. Instead, they are organized to clarify through insight and understand our ideas, ignite spiritual light for our inspiration and illumination and provide an emotionally safe, neutral environment where it's easier for us to recognize and accept truths about ourselves.

How the Akasha Works

The Akasha is the light that illuminates and ignites wisdom and compassion embedded in the Soul. When we open our Records, this light energy flows down from our eighth chakra. Chakras are invisible energy centers that organize the flow of the life force though us, manage the reception of life energies both within and beyond us, and distribute the force to unseen internal channels where it can be utilized. There are seven major chakras within the core of the human body, starting at the base or root of the spine, and continuing up through the body to the top of the head. While they cannot be seen with the human eye, spiritual sensitives throughout the ages have been able to detect these portals, and discern the particular role each plays in our growth and development.

Don't stress if you have never heard about the chakras. They work beautifully, with or without our attention. While it can be helpful to have a general understanding of their existence and role, a full course of study is not required. For our purposes, we most need to know about the eighth chakra, which resides approximately 18 inches above the crown of the head. This is the location where our individual Souls become distinct, although not separate from, the one Universal Soul. The eighth chakra is a point of intersection of your Soul, you as an individual being, and your earthly life. Here you may detect the presence of a horizon of light that is infinite and eternal, spanning all directions. As this light enters the crown of our head, it lands in our heart center, bounces off the floor of the heart and radiates out horizontally. As the light moves through us, it naturally converts to love, possibly activating emotions or even physical sensations.

While this Akashic light pours through us, we want to keep in mind that we are already light at the center of our being; we are not empty vessels being filled up by an outside force. Instead, we are infused with light at the level of individual atoms. Entering into the Akashic Records ignites the light that is already, and has always been, present within. It reminds me of hitting the "refresh" button on the computer, bringing the page to the most updated version available. Taking your place consciously within your own Records causes a quickening in the Akashic Field, sending a wake-up call to every expression of you that's ever been, and to who you are becoming. It is the case of light seeking and finding light, throughout time and space. Such is the power of conscious awareness. First, the energy is transmitted, then the information. A small percentage of people (5%) report hearing something, 10% say they see images, and most of us (85%) experience a sense of knowing.

The Akashic Records are a vibrational archive of every Soul and its journey, the memory of lifetimes and incarnations of humans within the context of our earthly existence. Everyone without exception is included in the Records. The Records pertain to humans on earth, but do not serve extraterrestrials or galaxies (in other words, this is not a resource for exploring life on other planets). You can think of it as the "cosmic memory of earthly life" centering on humans. The Record does not address trans-species activity, the phenomena of moving from animal to human to mineral, and the like. It does not say what is valid or invalid. It does not concern itself with this issue. Additionally, the Record is everywhere, present both within and beyond us. Never is it necessary to travel to a particular location on earth to make this connection. The relationship is perceptual, and is easily invigorated with a slight shift in awareness. Even the smallest amount of the Akashic Field contains the whole, a structural paradox much like a hologram.

Each person's Record has two parts. The first is the "blueprint of the Soul," our ultimate potential. Even though "blueprint" implies a tangible visual map, the Record is vibrational and invisible. No one literally sees a blueprint—this is just a metaphor. You and I each have a sacred trust of potential, which we recognize and realize as we live our incarnations. At some stage of our Soul's journey, we awaken to our ultimate potential, and accept and express that. Whether it takes 20 or 2,000 lifetimes matters not, for we are infinite beings within eternity.

Traveling alongside the Soul's blueprint is the catalog of the lifetimes through which we become aware of our potential and manifest it while in human form. It's natural to share our magnificence when we are in a nonphysical, body-free state, but being able to identify and express our deeper truths while we live our lives wrapped in issues of mortgages, teenagers and aging parents is challenging.

Our mission is to identify our potential (our Soul's Purposes) and find ways to bring them into the world. Within the greater context of growing into unconditional self- love, complete acceptance of others and appreciation of earthly life.

The Akasha is composed of the primary substance of the Universe, and is malleable, responding to our thoughts, feelings and actions. This is ground zero for manifesting—the region where our consciousness engages with life to bring forth our truths. Consider the Akashic Field a reservoir of essential life substance awaiting interaction with your awareness to generate tangible expression. Within the Akashic Field, manifestation is born.

The very best way I know to access the Akashic Field is through the Pathway Prayer Process@ to Access the Heart of the Akashic Records. The Prayer is especially effective for making a more conscious connection with your Soul. In a few chapters, you will have a chance to learn the basics. You know you already have a relationship with your own Soul, but you will have an opportunity to enjoy an even deeper awareness. But first, let's explore the power of our Soul's Purposes and understand their important role in manifestation.

4

The Compelling Power of Soul's Purposes

Whether consciously aware of it or not, you are always manifesting—bringing your Soul's Purposes to life—usually along with a combo platter of old ideas, fears, assumptions, and confusion. As you encounter new experiences, your thoughts may change, raising questions, rearranging ideas, opening up to possibilities, and your physical everyday world may even change to more accurately represent your emerging state of awareness. Realizing that you prefer a different destination may indicate it's time to act in a new way, and that's where this work enters the picture. You are already generating something—but what if you could more authentically manifest what you deeply desire in ways that are useful and fulfilling?

It's true that we have tremendous influence and power to exercise choice over our own experiences. While we are each the author of our own personal realm, none of us is the ultimate authority of the entire universe. And it is also true that we are each a requisite piece of the whole. To embrace this seeming paradox, imagine you are driving a speedboat on Lake Michigan. As the captain of the boat, you have authority over the vehicle. The better you understand how the machine operates, the better you can perform as its driver.

Next, consider how much you understand about the water the boat is moving in. Identifying the properties of the water supports your ability to navigate. Finally, explore the relationship of the boat to the water. While you have no authority over the water, your understanding of its nature and its relationship to your speedboat will help you successfully navigate the trip.

So it is with navigating our human self on the ocean of life. How we self-manage within the stream of life increases our understanding of life. In fact, this is the key area of our power. Many of us have dedicated tremendous energy to the outside world (the lake, using the metaphor of water above), while others have placed our attention on our inner terrain (the boat). Our current opportunity is to examine the realm where outer and inner dimensions intersect, so that we can activate the potential for preferred consequences.

The region where we self-express our emerging identity intersects with life, and life responds—each constantly adapting to achieve a harmonious relationship—is the Realm of Engagement. Our growth and development occur within this Realm. Our universe demands transformation within a context of change. Once in a lifetime events do occur, but rarely, and often as part of a larger pattern. We are always in flux, either changing or resisting change.

My Soul's Purposes in Action

Over the past 40 years, I've enjoyed the sacred opportunity to apply spiritual principles to my own life, to discover their true meaning, reveal hidden assumptions, and find the sweet spot. I have noticed that when spiritual ideas intersect with living my human life, miracles inevitably result. I happen to be a dramatic person, which I've come to appreciate as a very effective manner for identifying the patterns playing out in my life. And it's obvious to others, such as friends and family, who quickly recognize the confusion of my assumptions, and their own connections with my perspectives.

One of my most startling nudges happened years ago, when I was living in a studio apartment in Chicago. I loved the building and the location was ideal but, after a few years, I wanted a larger space. It occurred to me that I could apply spiritual principles to this situation. After a bit of reading and attending spirituality classes, I came upon an appealing notion. My understanding of it was to regularly declare my intention, then act as if I was already in my ideal home, and then the Universe would respond by meeting my demands. You may already know how this story ends.

With enthusiasm, I ventured out—buoyed by limitless faith, but working with limited funds. Within a week, I was the proud tenant of a lovely one-bedroom unit in my ideal building. Bliss ensued. Continuing to check my bank balance— expecting the necessary funds to be deposited there by the conspiring Universe—I saw, instead, soaring expenses. Rent was coming due. Inevitably, I faced the fact that my income was not increasing to meet the increased cost of living, and had to move out of my fantasy situation into a flat with roommates, in a place nowhere near the best neighborhood. Overextended beyond my means, past my beliefs, I found myself living in a far less desirable place than my original studio. Bewildered, I wrestled to figure out what went wrong. I had followed the "rules" but "the Universe" hadn't responded according to my plans. Truth be told, I've heard hundreds of stories just like this, where blind faith, confusion, and naiveté led to disappointment, anger, and upset.

Manifesting becomes a lifelong process when we relate with the world in which we live—as it is—in a harmonious dance that becomes a reciprocal, mutually enhancing exchange of resources. As curious explorers, we surrender to and trust life, knowing our external world is an expression of our own internal truth, aware of our interconnectedness. Trusting is not a passive waiting. In fact, trust builds as we take action. Exploration and experimentation expand awareness. As our awareness expands and our expectations shift, we gather momentum. An incremental growth process begins, fueling our ability to maneuver inevitable hardships and challenges. We participate, trusting in life, without any guarantees, or need for perfection. We act without needing to know. In fact, waiting for perfection stifles us from starting. Insisting on "figuring it out" first is not a spiritual approach.

Assumptions in the Age of Awakening

Spiritual Awareness

In the current tsunami of climate change, political unrest and endless new technological discoveries, individuals on every continent, in every walk of life, sense a troubling incongruence in their lives. Although we live in the Age of Information, our minds are flooded daily with more answers than we can possibly process, this is the time to ask questions. While uncertainty abounds, awakening souls are compelled to discover the certainty of truth. Despite being more connected by the worldwide web than ever before, we yearn for deeper connections. Regardless of unprecedented material wealth, we are eager to express all the spiritual treasures we hold. Fortunately, a new spirituality is emerging to meet these challenging paradoxes.

Making a few assumptions will provide a foundation for this new spirituality. Chief among them is the radical notion that all people are essentially good. Since all people are basically virtuous, everyone is equally worthy of enjoying the blessings of the human experience. Ancient hierarchies (with solid lines of demarcation between those who are deserving, and those who are undeserving) no longer apply here. We are all equally deserving of the best life has to offer. This idea alters the way we think about manifesting. It is no longer the exclusive domain of noble birth, economic privilege or educational advantage. It is now the birthright of all people, from every walk of life, every socio-economic group. Manifestation is the natural consequence of our consciousness, leaving no exclusions or exceptions to Inspired Manifesting. The spectacular opportunity for each and every person is to determine what's most important, and proceed with the inner work of cultivating beliefs and interpretations to support these heartfelt desires.

Akashic Assumptions

1. Everyone, always, without exception, is doing their very best.

Let me explain what I mean by "best." We are each motivated by a desire to increase our personal experience of being loved, feeling secure and at peace. At our core, our essence is love. As we come to recognize this truth about ourselves, it becomes obvious about others. We see that every person is love at their core and so, naturally, we don't have to send them love or light. And we never need to generate light from within (not that it's even possible). Simply, we are elegant, effective agents of light and love.

Our work is to clear the way so that these truths embedded in our hearts and souls can more easily find their way to the surface, so we can recognize, realize and express them. As we resolve our human challenges, the light at the center of our being is freed from all obstructions—and we shine! This brings about a wonderful result. As we make peace with our human selves by practicing acceptance for our perceived imperfections and appreciating our humanity, our magnificence emerges.

This doesn't mean that we always behave kindly, but our loving essence is central to our identity. Love can be experienced and expressed in countless ways. This assumption is rooted in the idea that the Divine resides within each of us, and also, that we are each individually responsible for our experience. Paradox plays an important role here. The ultimate spiritual paradox is that we are simultaneously infinite, eternal, immortal souls and finite, temporal, mortal humans.

Every action we ever take is an effort to provide love, peace and security. We are always doing our utmost best, without exception. All human beings throughout time have been striving to identify their number one choice, or best possible options. The criteria for these everyday decisions is this, "Will this choice increase my experience of being loved, feeling safe and having a peaceful mind?" People truly love themselves, and are in a valiant effort to take top-notch care as they live this life. No person ever opts for their third choice.

It is also true that obstructions to awareness of our immutable goodness exist. Our personal vulnerabilities are rooted in fear, anger and shame. But let's consider the possibility that our obstructions are actually in our best interest. If they were not beneficial for us, we would quickly and easily release them. In this softening phase of our awakening, we have the chance to be extremely kind and patient with ourselves, recognizing our noble motives coupled with our limited human capacities.

Our human selves are laden with troubling imperfections. The challenge is to accept ourselves as is and to allow our traits, characteristics and perceived imperfections to fall away, opening a space for the love within us to flow freely.

Acceptance is one of the most powerful, transformational tools at our disposal. To accept is to recognize the existing reality of something. Our approval is not required. As we allow the present reality of anything to exist, our relationship with that thing, whether person or condition, becomes much less antagonistic. Acceptance acts like Teflon, coating the surface of our emotional nerves, allowing things to be exactly the way they are, or the way they are not. In doing so, we make peace with unpleasant realities and, as we do, tension is released. As this tension is released, the way to grasp our next step opens. Acceptance facilitates release.

The opposite of this approach is negative judgment, which acts like Krazy Glue, keeping us stuck to difficult situations, and troubling people. Actively condemning and cursing anything is a guaranteed strategy to ensure that the two of you are bound and connected. Think twice before indulging in resentment. It ultimately weaves fierce bonds that are tricky to dissolve. Many of us were raised to glamorize criticism, sarcasm and mean-spirited banter as funny and smart. The truth is that this is crippling and painful, and not helpful on the path of awakening spiritual awareness.

2. Divine seeds of potential exist within us as our deepest dreams.

When these seeds activate, our longing for fulfilling our potential awakens. For the seeds to activate and change state, ignition is required. We need a spark for activation of potential, much like the heat of fire causes a state change. Consider that reading this book may stimulate a certain kind of spark within you, encouraging a change from one way of being to another. Your commitment to your spiritual journey—combined with this material—can stimulate a "fire of consciousness" activating your very own Divine seeds of potential. Do you feel an uncomfortable, exciting angst of awakening just reading these words?

The seeds of our ultimate potential are embedded into the fabric of our souls. Each one of us has our own individual packet of seeds. In the space of possibility, we become aware of our unique dreams, wishes and desires. You and I each have deeply seeded desires, the particulars of which are unique. If we asked a room of 500 people to share their heartfelt dreams, we would hear 500 different sacred ideas. Some may be in the same realm, but at the end of the day, each would be personally unique.

Thinking of this moves me to tears. The perfection of the Universe blows my mind. Every one of us has a part to play in this cosmic unfolding. And, each of us is required to do what is ours to do. As we become aware of our inner treasures and dreams, we are charged with the responsibility to bring these intentions to life, to manifest them. In the process of pursuing our Soul's Purposes, we naturally relinquish limitations of our personality, and ascend into our ultimate potential. The business of our Soul's Purposes is vital to the optimal transformation of the entire creation. Each of us doing our part catapults us into dimensions beyond our shortcomings, into a sphere of awareness and expression, infused with the finest aspects of our being, where we enjoy who we are and the whole of creation. This is something to reach for!

**3. In the Age of Awakening Spiritual Awareness,
the essential truth is this: we are one.
Each one of us is an integral part of life.**

Despite our illusion to the contrary, it's impossible to be separate from or outside of life. Yet more of us than ever before feel alone, blocked, isolated or some other interpretation of the myth of separation—an understanding that is based on a limiting belief. If we were exiled from life (an impossibility), we would cease to exist. The very fact that you are alive is evidence that you belong here.

The global awakening to our oneness happens on an individual level; it is accomplished one Soul at a time. We don't have role models, other than a few Ascended Masters such as Jesus, Buddha and Lao Tzu. And so it's up to us to embrace and embody this new worldview. As this awareness spreads, it becomes contagious to those open to this possibility. While someone can suggest this notion, no one can force it upon another. When it's time and we are receptive, the Light of Truth will find us and ignite our inner fire, expanding our awareness. Huge swaths of people on every continent are being internally prompted by their own Souls to recognize that there is more to life than the human eye can see—that there is a discernible presence both within and beyond them.

We live in times of epic change—within our relationships, ourselves, and with all of life. Across the board and around the world, people on every continent and in every culture and socio-economic group are being stimulated and expanding into new levels of awareness. Along with these new realms of consciousness come new ideas, understandings, interpretations and perspectives, giving us all an exceptional opportunity to review our standards. On a global scale, institutions, organizations, governmental entities, economic systems, religions and infrastructures are also undergoing dramatic revisions.

It's important not to underestimate the significance of the times in which we live, and the fact that we chose to be here for this experience. There are particular aspects of this transitional era that invite our deeper inspection and reflection. Within the context of tremendous fundamental change, we will look at some of the specific ideas morphing before our very eyes.

One major paradigm dissolving rapidly—thankfully, as it blocks Inspired Manifestation—is the idea that we are separate. When we are convinced that we are separate from all others, and a solitary creature unrelated to the life in which we find ourselves, we generate a collection of behaviors that validate our conviction. Our sense of isolation generates fear, and our fears pile up like bricks forming a wall surrounding us. This prevents others from direct contact with us, and keeps us from meaningful bonds with others. As we continue to experience separation, we gather evidence, strengthening our fears. Growing confusion fuels our justification to isolate more, and what started out to be protective walls become barriers to satisfying engagement with other people. As a result, we deprive ourselves of valuable interactions, hide our truth and push people away.

For those of us interested in Inspired Manifestation, this is particularly troubling, because life occurs through relationships. Everything, from events to experiences and measurable results in between, takes place through us as human beings. Manifesting transpires through us, not outside of or beyond us. Life does not deliver through clouds in the sky, or sprouts pushing up out of the earth. Rather, life reveals itself to us through us, and one another. It's the way of the world. And if we sincerely want to manifest our dreams, the first step is to recognize the reality of how our hopes and dreams take shape—through others in ordinary time and space. Any insistence that life alters its customary patterns to accommodate our requests will be disappointing. Fulfillment of our dreams happens within the context of planetary life.

While the tribal worldview (in the form of nationalism) thrashes around doing its best to survive, a more accurate recognition of interconnectedness is emerging (or you could say, re-emerging) in a paradigm of oneness. Long considered a religious ideal (and even longer known by indigenous people to be so), many are now waking up to realize that our reality is unity. Scientists prove this truth, philosophers explain it, mathematicians calculate it and economists experiment with alternate systems to reflect unity consciousness. I look forward to the resulting recognition of our oneness to save us from our tribal violence and destructive wars.

4. Every person alive—no matter what age, race, culture, or creed—bases every decision on a deep desire to increase their personal experience of love and enrich their sense of well-being, safety, belonging and value.

In real life, this often plays out in confusing ways. Curiously, our choices can occasionally cause harm—despite our motivation to increase our personal experience of being loved. For example, a normally calm parent may yell at a beloved child when overwhelmed, simply hoping that the child will stop misbehaving. The parent's intention is to regain composure and control over the situation even though, in exasperation, she may use words that end up hurting her child. The parent's intention is not to harm, but to restore her sense of peace.

Imagine what strategies an individual with a powerful presence on the world stage may employ when driven by a personal need to be loved. Initially, they may be accommodating, mediating on behalf of their constituents in a civilized manner. But, at some point, they may imagine that eliminating a particular minority group would resolve the issue. On every continent, in every era, world leaders have convinced themselves that problems are caused by scapegoats. When out of control, they engineer a mass elimination. Interviewing any one of history's tyrants would reveal their professed innocence, shedding light on valid (to them) reasons for their cruel behavior. As confounding as this assumption can be, it's a foundational principle. Even the most heinous act is motivated by a desire to achieve inner peace and outer love.

5. The Universe always provides enough of what we need to bring our Soul's Purposes to life.

There is enough for our very next step. This is because who we are is a part of the Universe. Of course, the Universe holds all the nuts and bolts of our potential. But, it is rare that we have all that we need for the entire project from the beginning. Our work is to take the next step and trust that we have just enough of what we need to move forward, even if we cannot see the entire path.

Speaking of moving forward, it's time to learn how to read your Akashic Records, using the remarkable Pathway Prayer Process©.

6

How to Read Your Own Akashic Records

Life offers unlimited ways to enrich our conscious connection with our spiritual awareness. You've likely discovered many along your path, as have I. Of all the avenues I have explored in my lifetime, I am most impressed with the Akashic Records. I still marvel at the role it has played in my personal transformation. My discovery began after a life-changing moment of spiritual awareness at the age of 24, which catapulted me into an expanded awareness of spiritual reality. Deeply moved, I found myself constantly seeking to duplicate the experience.

My search took 16 wonderful years until I was, at long last, led to the Akashic Records. Much to my surprise, my encounter in the Records was the closest replication of the original earlier event. Riveting magnetism drew me into a flow of Akashic Light and Presence. After seven years of productive exploration, what I now call "the Pathway Prayer Process" came to me. It facilitated a shift in my core connection with the Akasha, moving me from a mentally dominant practice to one anchored in the heart of the Akasha, where I enjoyed all the wonders of an unconditionally loving spiritual reality. Since that time, I've had the good fortune to share these practices and protocols with tens of thousands of students globally, and create a Doctorate in Spiritual Studies in the Akashic Records. This is far beyond my wildest imaginings!

Along the way, I have shared the wisdom of the Akasha with students in a variety of formats, including three prior books. My very first work, *How to Read the Akashic Records*, focuses on the method, the Prayer, how the Records are organized, how they function, what's reasonable to expect in this realm as well as foundational practices for energy healing, clearing ancestral patterns and past lives. In *Healing through the Akashic Records*, my second book, I address the issue of personal growth and transformation, covering the powerful processes for liberating yourself from limiting patterns, shifting attachments to wounding life experiences and the Ascension Matrix. By the time we arrive at book three, *Discover Your Soul's Path through the Akashic Records*, we are ready to turn our attention to our relationship with life itself, knowing one of the cherished ideals for many of us is to be able to maintain our spiritual awareness while living effectively in the world. All of this leads us to now and the task at hand—using the Akashic Records via the Pathway Prayer Process © to investigate our Soul's Purposes and facilitate our own Inspired Manifesting.

In my own experience, this spiritual path serves as an "on ramp" to a broad highway of light, love, peace and power. Noted for its inclusion for all people from every walk of life, race, culture, socio-economic group and age, this path continuously expands to make room for seekers of every stripe. This self-selecting group lives in a dynamic relationship of give and take from this all-inclusive yet non-invasive realm of consciousness. It contains all possibilities, probabilities and potentials for our recognition, discovery and application. This realm of raw spiritual essence is waiting to be mined to bring about the fulfillment of our Soul's Purposes. It is the optimal arena for Inspired Manifesting—the region where our authentic, Soul-level desires engage with the primary substance of life, where our spiritual vision connects with the raw materials to become manifest here on earth.

Whether you have worked in the Akashic Records before or not, I'm going to teach you everything you need to know about using the Records for the purposes of manifesting your Soul's Purposes. For me, personally, the Akasha has been the very best tool for helping me to access the spiritual perspective, Soul-level point of view; see and know myself and my challenges from the illuminated and inspired perspective of my Soul; and to align with the divine vision for my growth, transformation, and happiness.

This work has the potential to positively change your entire relationship with yourself and your life. The way we identify and interpret ourselves and life's events determines the quality of our experience. Our assumptions about human nature, and beliefs about the life force drive us to evaluations and decisions molding our path. Working in our own Akashic Records using the Pathway Prayer Process © provides a tremendous opportunity for us to connect with an essentially spiritual point of view, altering our individual trajectory to one of enhanced possibilities.

Before we begin, let's visit some important prerequisites. Here are the critical guidelines:

Guidelines for Reading Your Own Akashic Records

Do not consume drugs or alcohol for 24 hours before opening the Records. These substances weaken the edge of the energy field, and you will lose authority over your experience. You want to be clear, strong and responsible with your spiritual work. Drinking and drugs make us feel connected to people, which is okay in some situations, but not helpful when doing this work. Nicotine, caffeine, and sugar do not affect this work, but please pay attention to portion size before doing a reading.

Use your current legal name when opening the Records. Every name has a vibration. We are calling forth the vibrational archive of your Soul. Be sure to use your current legal name, not your birth name.

Be responsible for your time in the Records. Know before entering how long you plan to stay. Ten minutes is a good minimum, one hour is the max. In the beginning, don't spend longer than 30 minutes. Your own energy needs to remain strong, and it takes practice to build your "spiritual muscle" in the Records. When I'm working in my own Records, I tell myself I am going to be doing this for 20 or 30 minutes. When disciplined about the structure, we can go deeper.

Ground yourself after each reading. Do something that reminds you that you are a human being: water the plants, go outside, walk the dog, talk to the kids, call your mother. Pay attention to this opportunity to get in touch with yourself, and connect with the life you are living.

When combining the Akashic Records with another system, always honor both systems. After the first 30 days of practice, when you are more familiar with this energy and how it affects you, you may wish to consider mixing this with another complementary method. Some people like to add this practice to Reiki, Feng Shui, astrology, etc.

To stimulate this connection, use the Pathway Prayer Process© set forth below. Remember, the connection is always in place; we are activating our awareness of this already-existing relationship. Saying the Prayer according to the instructions causes a simple shift in our attention—from ordinary to extraordinary. This means that we have expanded our ability to perceive what is already present. Consider it like turning the lights on in a dim room. The contents of the room remain the same but our vision is enhanced. As we use the Prayer, we experience a subtle shift in our awareness so that it is easier to recognize, whether visually, audibly or emotionally, the elements of our situation, the emotional atmosphere and after some acclimation, the essential truth of our challenge. We are always awake and aware, fully conscious. There is no need to worry about being ambushed by some unknown forces, no worries about being unable to recall the truth. We are present, and able to describe what is happening, or not, as the case may be.

Imagine you are wandering around a house with lousy lighting. It's a lovely place, but you can't seem to get clarity on the place or its contents and, consequently, it's extremely difficult to determine if this is a place you want to be or not. Saying the Prayer is like turning on the lights, so you can better identify the place and your experience, without any negative judgment or condemnation. With the added benefit of the light of Infinite Truth, Wisdom and Compassion, the nuts and bolts of our lives take on greater value, and we are naturally able to make conscious choices on our own behalf. It is deceptively simple, yet profound.

When we say the Opening Prayer, the metaphorical light goes up and then dims, as you recite the Closing Prayer. But, we know that the truth once recognized is never forgotten. You will always have the impression of the highest interpretation of yourself and your situation. It cannot be lost. In this space of infinite light and love, it's easier to be honest with ourselves about our motives, desires and vulnerabilities. There's nothing to fear.

And now it's time for me to share with you a magnificent and powerful prayer.

THE PATHWAY PRAYER PROCESS@
TO ACCESS THE HEART OF THE AKASHIC RECORDS

Opening Prayer

And so we do acknowledge the Forces of Light,
Asking for guidance, direction, and courage to know the Truth
As it is revealed for our highest good and the highest good of everyone connected to us.
Oh Holy Spirit of God, Protect me from all forms of self-centeredness
And direct my attention to the work at hand.
Help me to know *myself* in the Light of the Akashic Records,
To see *myself* through the eyes of the Lords of the Records,
And enable me to share the wisdom and compassion that the Masters, Teachers, and Loved Ones of *me* have for *me*.

The Records are now open.

Closing Prayer

I would like to thank the Masters, Teachers, and Loved Ones for their love and compassion.
I would like to thank the Lords of the Akashic Records for their point of view.
And I would like to thank the Holy Spirit of Light for all knowledge and healing.

The Records are now closed. Amen.
The Records are now closed. Amen.
The Records are now closed. Amen.

TO OPEN YOUR OWN RECORDS

So, here's how it works. Read the first three stanzas aloud, and then read the stanza beginning with "Help me" twice, silently to yourself, using your current legal name. When finished, announce, "The Records are now open" aloud. When dealing with alternate states of consciousness, following the directions is important as they strengthen our ability to go deeper by being very clear about where we are. You will see that there are two parts to the Prayer: an opening and a closing.

Use both. In the Opening Prayer, there are three stanzas, each with a specific purpose. The purpose of the first stanza is the Invocation; we are calling in the light. When praying, it is always a good idea to know who you are praying to. We are calling the Forces of light and asking for guidance, direction, and courage to know the Truth. This is a very co-creative process.

In our second stanza, we enter conscious alignment with the Spirit of God. It is also our protection. From a Records' standpoint, everything in life is for us; everything is supporting us somehow. The only thing that can really cause us serious trouble is our own self-centeredness. You can bet that our self-centered fears will take us down. If I am going into my Records and I'm worried about myself, I'm not going anywhere. My Prayer is to protect me from all forms of self-centeredness because if anything will get in the way, that's going to be it. "And direct my attention to the work at hand" is about assuming a posture of service. It's very powerful, like opening a channel so that more can come.

Now, in our third stanza, we are petitioning. We want to see ourselves through the eyes of the Lords of the Records. "Enable me to share the wisdom and compassion..." After working in the Records, we close by reading the entire Closing Prayer out loud. It's simply saying, "Thank you" with "The Records are now closed. Amen." Repeating this three times helps establish ourselves in ordinary reality.

This standard process was revealed to me through working in my own Records, and has proven to be a reliable map for those desiring life-changing readings for themselves. When you first start using it, you may feel a bit awkward, but keep trying. Once you are more comfortable, it will be significantly easier for you to explore any issues weighing on you, and arrive at inspiring solutions. I suggest you take it on as a spiritual practice. For the next week or so, spend some time each day in your Akashic Records. Notice what happens. Reflect and record your insights.

It's a good idea to give yourself a chance to practice the Pathway Prayer Process©. Being able to identify the energies and how they affect you is best done over time, through practice. Luckily for most of us, there's no need to be psychic or clairvoyant. If you are, it's very helpful to have some experience using the Pathway Prayer Process© so you can distinguish the ways in which it's similar and different for you. The rest of us can just experiment with the Prayer, learn how it works, strengthen our relationship with it and apply the recommendations.

Positive results are the best way to cultivate a powerful connection with the Records. Take your time, and remember this is not an oracle for divination, but a tool to empower our spiritual awareness. Then we have an incredible opportunity to be inspired by pure Akashic Light. All of these steps help us prepare for our spiritual awakening, as we come to know the spiritual nature of our Soul.

Now that you've learned what you need to know about the Akashic Records, feel free to continue your exploration of Inspired Manifestation by opening your Records. Keep in mind that this is a form of spiritual counseling, offering insight, guidance and wisdom rooted in unconditional love. Enjoy the quest.

POWER PROTOCOL

In every Akashic Records reading, there are three levels to consider, whether we are problem solving to get away from a difficulty, or struggling to move forward toward a personal dream. The circumstances dictate which level is emphasized. People come to me for readings because they have temporarily forgotten that the light is within them—they have forgotten their own goodness. Perhaps they cannot reconcile their life circumstances, or they are using what is happening in their lives against themselves, like a weapon (my mate left me, which must mean I am terrible). I apply the Power Protocol, shining Akashic light on the challenge at hand to view it through the spiritual lens of unconditional love.

This perspective is absolutely transformational. It changes us, along with our interpretations and judgments, and accelerates our ability to relinquish unnecessarily harsh understandings. Love can then rise up and inform our point of view. The three levels of the Power Protocol are: Story, Causes and Conditions, and Soul-level Truth (who you are is good, no matter what you have or haven't done). Here are the considerations at each level:

1. **Story.** What is happening? Or not happening? Identify the concern. It's best to describe what's occurring, and the impact it's having on you. No need to try to figure things out at this level. Simply tell the story of what's going on, and how you are being affected. Acceptance is the great spiritual opportunity at this point. To the best of your ability, set aside your opinions about yourself, and the situation in which you find yourself.

2. **Causes and Conditions.** This is the part of the process where we explore and examine all the valid reasons we are in this situation. We entertain the question, "Why?" And begin to consider some possible reasons. They may be past life, inherited from prior lifetimes or related to our childhood or family of origin. Seeking and finding the valid reasons for selections we made, placing us in our current circumstances is the first part of our spiritual opportunity at this stage. We recognize that we are always in the process of trying to secure more love and peace for ourselves, and every choice we make is motivated by our desire

for love. It's very helpful to understand why we believed that our decision would bring us an enhanced experience of love. The second part of this is to raise the turbo-charged healing question to ourselves, "How do I love and respect myself, even though I'm in this undesirable, possibly terrible, situation?" How is it possible to extend kindness, mercy, patience and understanding to myself while I'm in the midst of this unresolved matter?"

3. **Soul-level Truth.** This part of the process is especially exciting. Here we are challenged to take a leap in awareness. Here we strive to see, sense, or "get" that we are undeniably perfect at the level of our soul. There is a light of love and goodness that is the core of who we are, which is unaffected by our human imperfections. When working in the Records, we can invite some assistance to recognize these truths about ourselves. The Soul-level Truth about you is that you are very loving, wonderful even though you are facing a troublesome reality. Your Soul cannot be polluted or corrupted, stolen or given away. It is yours, and the love comprising your very nature persists in the midst of human challenges. Even when stressed out, confused, heartbroken or sick, you are able to love, to give, to enjoy, to share and appreciate that essential love is unhampered. This recognition of your own unalterable goodness is unconditional love in action, the highest spiritual practice available to us all. At this level of the reading, you have a sense of appreciating yourself, no matter what. You are on your own side, and you know it. Our personal awareness of our infinite goodness is what ignites a shift in our relationship with our difficulties. This transformation is the foundation for any resulting healing or changes that come to pass. Without it, there is scant growth or change.

The following practice is designed to be done using the Pathway Prayer Process© to Access the Heart of the Akashic Records. For best results, follow the protocol for opening and closing your Akashic Records.

REFLECTION: AKASHIC PRESENCE

Open Your Akashic Records using the Pathway Prayer Process©. Occupy this sacred space as if you are the filament within your own light bulb, because you are. Open up to the always supportive, never intrusive or invasive, presence of your Masters, Teachers and Loved Ones. Sometimes they feel like they'll catch me if I lean back, while at other times I sense that they are ahead of me, beckoning me to take my next steps, even though they cannot be seen. At still other times, it's as if I'm in the company of forever best friends sharing the journey, walking shoulder-to-shoulder through time and space. When facing a thorny issue, I recognize them as my most trusted spiritual advisors, ready to shine Akashic light on my confusion to bring the spiritual potential into focus. I cannot see them, but I know they are leading and prompting me into who I am becoming. Such is the nature of their work.

KEY CONCEPTS FOR PRODUCTIVE ENGAGEMENT
IN YOUR OWN RECORDS

There are a handful of ideas I want to share with you that can make a decisive difference when venturing into the Akashic Field for spiritual support. One of the most impressive observations I've encountered is that people with an interest in using the Records naturally have the ability to be successful. This is a spiritual practice, not a magic formula. It develops over time. While you may be brimming with natural ability, your corresponding skills may need some attention. I like to think in terms of an oil well. The earth is swollen with crude oil, but if we can't reach it with the right tools, it goes untapped. Such is the case with spiritual gifts. While they live within each of us, our conscious application and delivery of them dramatically increases their value. Only people who have the ability to work in the Records have the desire. Relax and let yourself learn the best ways to connect with your infinite inner spiritual resources.

The purpose of doing readings is to access the spiritual perspective, the Soul-level point of view. When opening the Records, we have the sacred opportunity to consider and comprehend ourselves from the illumined, inspired, unconditionally loving perspective of the Soul. Additionally, recognizing and understanding our human challenges from this vantage point. Ultimately, this perspective nurtures our ability to consciously align with the Ultimate/Divines vision of ourselves, for our personal growth, transformation and fulfillment. When someone inquires about a reading, I tell them that, "We look at who you are and the challenges you're facing from the Soul-level perspective, the lens of unconditional love." Our attention is always on the person we wish to serve, in this case, ourselves and recognizing the presence of love, no matter what is transpiring.

Because the Record is a space of light and love, it is spiritual rather than psychic. The good news for most of us is that you do not have to be psychic or "clair" anything—not clairaudient, clairvoyant, or clairsentient, to do meaningful work in your Records. As an archive of the Soul, the Record is available to anyone with a Soul, which includes us all, without exception. But, we know not everyone is interested in this type of pursuit as we all have different gifts and interests. While anyone with a desire to engage in the Records is welcome, each discovers their own strengths and natural abilities once acclimated. You are inherently spiritual, and welcome in the field of pure light.

As a realm of light, there is no need to pray to the Records or its managing light being members. We do not worship or implore the Akasha. The light is always on our side, shining on us no matter our circumstances, character flaws or confusion. What can be slippery for many of us is adjusting to this concept and reality of being totally accepted, known and loved all the time. For many of us, it's directly opposite our human experience, and takes a bit of time for us to adjust to this new reality.

The Akashic Records are governed by Three Absolutes—Fear Not, Judge Not and Resist Not—each supporting a spiritual space of sanctuary, reverence, kindness, respect, and compassion. These governing principles safeguard the realm, maintaining the sanctity of the Akashic Atmosphere. This Atmosphere is characterized by qualities of love. The essence of love and light is the bedrock of the Akashic Realm, and this love and light are expressed and experienced by us as recognizable attributes of love, differentiated by the needs of various individuals, meeting our requirements for particular aspects of love. For example, my son recently moved out and, even though it's a wonderful, happy event, I am sad that my little boy is now grown. When I go into my Records, I'm greeted with comfort and understanding, which go directly to my needs at this time. Other excursions bring different expressions of love, depending on my human needs in different circumstances. This is a remarkable feature of the Akashic Field. It naturally responds in the most appropriate ways to our basic human weaknesses, driving us along our path.

We've all heard that all truth lives within, and there's great wisdom in this idea. I recall many times my exasperated friends, doing their best, tried to redirect me to look within, since all the answers are there. No doubt this is accurate, but the issue for me became how? How do I get to that inner region, where inspired insight is waiting for me? As I've learned, we need an emotionally safe space to allow those inner treasures, embedded in our Souls, to emerge.

As true visionaries, we have two challenges. One is to allow our heart's desires to emerge, to let ourselves know the truth. Visions are treasures in our hearts we are often afraid to look at. As we're more understanding, accepting, patient and kind with ourselves, these precious nuggets can come into focus. And once we find awareness, we need to live our way into the realization of our vision.

Fortunately for us, instantaneous manifestation is rare. It is far more typical for us to grow into our visions, strengthening our human abilities to support the expression of our visions. What's surprisingly beneficial for the demonstration of our sacred dreams is ordinary human stability. I used to think that my deficiency was light and that, by generating more light, life would unfold effortlessly. I was wrong on a few counts. First, as a human I am unable to manufacture light, which is why my attempts in this area have been so frustrating. Instead, I've found that all the light of life already exists. It's already, and has always been here, within me (and you) at this exact moment in time, no matter where we happen to be. What's in the way is my confusion, clouding the reality of this situation. As it turns out, the more stable we are as people, the greater our ability to allow and accommodate the light to flow through us. This stability rests in the lower chakras.

At the core of our being, there is a pillar of light holding the energy centers, which correspond to different parts of us and the world:

- From the Root to the Crown Chakra is an inner pillar of light.
- At the base is the Root Chakra, the gateway to this incarnation, which holds the birth patterns of all incarnations.
- The Second Chakra, just below the belly button, is a center for spirituality, creativity, and sexuality—the varieties of pleasure and enrichment emanating from each.
- The Third Chakra, underneath our heart, is our self-worth.
- The Eighth Chakra is the point in space where the individual soul distinguishes (but never separates) itself from the Universal Soul.
- The Crown Chakra represents transition, death.

Consider, if you will, yourself as a chalice with a flat, secure base resting on the earth plane. Holding the stem solid and strong, reach upward to support the placement of a wide-open cup. Open at the top, this cup can receive and provide space for ideas of every variety to gather and combine within the chalice. A strong base and stem easily accommodate all kinds of activities, as light and truth interact with ideas, old and new, true and false until enlightened truth comes into sight. This is how the transformational process proceeds within. Our part is to fortify the stabilizing features so the light and wisdom within can reorganize to meet our current needs.

7

The Soul's Spiritual Nature: A Spiritual Awakening

As spiritual beings incarnated in physical bodies, we are on a quest. The purpose of our Soul's journey is to grow into an experience and expression of unconditional love. We have plenty of religious language in sacred texts, but what is the language of Soul? Our human journey is spiritual—but what exactly does that mean, and how does it significantly change the game? In a time of such a spiritual awakening as this, much is emerging, our understandings and interpretations are open-ended. When we prejudge the impact and value of our life occurrences, we shut the door on our own growth. I invite you to reject the urge to systematize the spiritual nature of your being. Allow yourself to be in the inquiry of the spiritual nature of your Soul. Let your questions be your guides.

The questions we carry in our hearts are clues to what's possible for us in this lifetime. Hints about our values, dreams and desires can be gleaned in the inquiries we find fascinating. Your natural curiosity about life and its multiple dimensions of activities and ideas—from the simple everyday quality of life, to the cosmic concerns guiding your attention and subsequent actions in this lifetime. Through our normal desire to be safe, included and loved, along with being able to contribute in some way, are all the seeds of manifesting our Soul's Purposes. While the fundamental impetus to be a vital part of our world is shared among us all, the specific, unique manner is different for each of us. Our individual expression of the universal life force is one of the keys igniting our manifestation.

Something exists within each of us that humans have sensed since the beginning of time. We cannot see it with our eyes or touch it with our hands, but we all emphatically agree that it exists. On every continent, through every age, human beings have ventured out into the world—or deep within themselves—to discover more about the spiritual nature of their existence. We have detected the presence of something greater than ourselves, as well as an intimate, sacred realm—our inner landscape. All cultures, religions, philosophies and belief systems have attempted to locate and name this elusive, eternal force. Humans have organized schools to explore this mystery, and developed devotional practices and rituals to touch it. And always, there are skeptics who refuse to recognize the non-rational, illogical realm, even considering us seekers to be immature, needy or just plain crazy.

It's helpful to consider that some lifetimes are devoted to expanding our conscious awareness of our spiritual awareness. During other incarnations, our focus rests in other areas of life, as it needs to be. There are phases of our growth, intense and demanding, yielding great adjustments in our perceptions and comprehension of life's mysteries, followed by lifetimes synthesizing our inner knowing with our human condition, so we can be grounded, integrated beings. We all have our turn at skepticism, doubt and spiritual suspicion, usually followed by enthusiasm and the embracing of profound, cosmic truth. I like to try not to get too worked up over a combination of attitudes in the collective response to burgeoning spiritual growth. The long view—I'm talking about a series of incarnations here— helps reduce any sting and keeps things in perspective.

After centuries of searching on every continent, from every

point of view—from religious to scientific and even superstitious—most of us agree that something exists that is remarkably closer to us than our own breath, and even more vast than the entire Universe. Something we all share access to awaits our awareness, acceptance, and appreciation—even though we experience and express it in unique ways. My great hope in this book is to facilitate your increased awareness of this ineffable essence, so that you can experience it within your inner world, and express it through your unique individuality, and participate in the magnificent symphony of life, knowing you are a critical and necessary part of the whole. In fact, the whole symphony of life awaits your contribution, your Inspired Manifesting.

Sometimes, we humans feel that our participation is insignificant and unimportant. In some cultures and traditions, it's considered noble and virtuous to diminish our desire to step up and help out. Others suggest that it's more spiritual to minimize our personal participation. And some consider it shameful or sinful to be conscious of our gifts and talents. Thank goodness we are here in this new age of awakening spiritual awareness, where we understand that the whole is composed of its parts and, without us, the world is a different place. Life is actually made up of all of us, each and every one, personal opinions notwithstanding, we are all in this together. And, this is good! Life needs us to do our part, no matter what we think, to bring realization of the universal Soul's Purposes to life. This is the trajectory for Inspired Manifesting.

What is the Nature of Spirituality?

Initially embarking on this path, I was confused about the meaning of spiritual growth. What is the relationship between religion and spirituality? Spirituality and superstition? What is the true nature of spirituality? Since this is a book about spirituality, let's clarify my understanding. As I've come to know it, spirituality is an invisible, eternal, unlimited, intimate, imminent, quality of aliveness that is life itself. It is an inherent, immutable aspect of every creature and element of creation. As we become awake to the presence of spirit, our co-creative partnership comes to life, empowering us to bring the hidden treasures of our inner being to life. The nature of spirit is love, an indestructible presence since the beginning of time. The spiritual domain is a loving aspect that we cannot diminish or delete.

Necessarily, spirit is only accessible to us as we become aware of its existence. The purpose of any spiritual practice is to deepen our conscious connection with life, to stimulate our awareness of the infinite within. Beyond theory, experience is required. We live on a plane of action; it's a critical element in our journey. Individual human awareness of the spiritual dimension and reality of ordinary life is an emerging process, not a singular event. There is a completely natural and seamless relationship between our spiritual nature and our human self. Life is both spiritual and material. Yet, in the early days of my awakening to spiritual awareness, I mistakenly believed that I had transcended my human form and entered into a realm far from human concerns. In fact, I had not stepped outside of my physical reality at all. I had awakened to a greater truth, that every part of human existence is inherently spiritual.

Spiritual Awakening

By spiritual awakening, I mean expanding awareness of this unseen reality. Awakening increases our conscious awareness. When a spiritual awakening is authentic, our relationship with who we are and with all of life becomes amplified, loving awareness. The purpose of a personal spiritual awakening is to experience and express the unconditional love living at the core of our being, and to enjoy our unique usefulness in the world. Increasingly, we know that we are love itself, existing within a palpable ocean of love.

Spiritual Practices

A spiritual practice is any repeated activity that makes it easier for us

to discern and detect the spiritual truth of infinite love within ourselves and beyond us. When we consciously, responsibly and deliberately connect with the Soul-level point of view, we begin to know
ourselves from a divine perspective, and see that we cannot be discon-
nected or separate from Soul. When engaging in a spiritual practice,
we can sense the presence of unconditional love and its particular expressions (respect, kindness, mercy and appreciation). Searching for
opportunities to experience unconditional love is the pinnacle of spiritual practice.

As we have our own experience of the unlimited reservoir of
love within, we naturally respond in ways that represent our individuality. We find activities, people and situations within which our awareness of the infinite body of love living in our hearts becomes active.
This activity causes love to expand, flow and fill us up so much that we
are compelled to share and express ourselves. Think of this as the inner
crucible, within which Inspired Manifesting begins.

For years, we have thought of spiritual practices in religious
terms—prayer, meditation, yoga, Taizé, tai chi—but there's more to
this. Any regular activity that keeps us aware of Soul, the spark of
spirit alive within us and around us, qualifies as a spiritual practice.
Life is exploding with opportunities for us to discover what inspires
feelings of love and happiness! I meditate with a mantra and pray
daily, but there are other activities, such as ice skating and baking,
that also remind me of the boundless reservoir of love and happiness.
My spiritual practices make me happy for no logical reason. One of
the hallmarks of an authentic spiritual practice is an inexplicable state
of happiness, characterized by true fulfillment and deep satisfaction.
Designed to unleash the infinite love that is the core of our being,
spiritual practice naturally propels us into the heart of the inherent
goodness of life. Consequently, we are happier. If your current engagement with spirit does not uplift or encourage you, it may be time to
discover something new.

Our spiritual practices can be understood as the links between
our Soul's needs and desires, as outlined by its blueprint, and the

world in which we live. The deepest desires of the Soul, essentially spiritual or loving, are nudging us to find ways to experience and express love as the person we are at this point in history. This is a segment of our Soul's journey throughout time. Our challenge is to identify the particulars of what ignites us now, and to take those actions.

When we think of an architectural blueprint, it can give us some clues about this process. This blueprint is an outline of what can be built. It's a description of the dream, the possibility for a specific building. Looking at the drawing, we get clarity about what actions to take that will bring us our result. It's quite the same with the soul's blueprint. Except for the fact that the Soul's blueprint is invisible, the principle is the same. In your heart of hearts lives a plan for who you will ultimately become throughout your lifetimes. Within each incarnation, different sections of the blueprint can be constructed based on your human talents, gifts and abilities within that life. These elements come into our awareness as simple desires for human experiences. We may find that we desperately, though inexplicably, want to teach history. It makes little sense, especially considering that we are surrounded with folks involved in other pursuits. But, we notice that no matter what happens in our lives, the nagging desire to teach history doesn't fade. And so, in spite of peer pressure to the contrary, we launch into a career as a history teacher. It turns out that we love it. It's fun, exciting, stimulating and hard work. It's all fabulous. Along the way, we find ourselves more loving, open, thoughtful and enjoying life beyond anything we imagined. This is what happens with the Soul's Purposes, blueprint, spiritual practices and our follow-through. It is through these very mundane parts of life that we find our way to our own personal Inspired Manifestation.

A Word About What is NOT Spiritual

When I feel the need to consult a psychic, it's because I want to know what's going to happen, and how I can manipulate the situation favorably, because I am afraid. There's nothing wrong with this nonspiritual approach, but there is a world of difference between psychic talents, and spiritual sensitivity. Any attempt to know the future to avoid the inconvenience and discomfort of being human is a weak expression of spiritual power.

Somewhere along the line, some of us adopted the notion that we would earn the coveted prize of supernatural abilities by being spiritual. Recently, I spoke with a client suffering tremendous disappointment because he had not acquired supernatural qualities after a lifetime as a vegan, meditating as much as possible. He believed he would eventually earn valuable gifts such as seeing auras, predicting future events, recalling past lives and channeling spirits. None of these came his way. Instead, he was left with increasing sensitivity to the feelings and needs of others, which he resented, and an expanding awareness of the goodness in everyone he encountered, which he appreciated. I understood his dismay. I, too, had once hoped that a lifetime of practice would produce a cornucopia of psychic phenomena to entertain and delight my clients.

Fortunately, we need not be psychics nor rely on supernatural abilities. As glamorous as they may be at times, they can also be a terrible distraction when we are on a spiritual quest, and that is exactly what we're doing. The spiritual can be so unassuming, it's easy to overlook. But, it's the path of power, aliveness, peace and harmony, all of which are commanding in their own right. Let's dive in now for a deeper exploration of your Soul's Purposes.

Processes to Manifest Your Soul's Purposes

When transforming consciousness, deliberate inquiry is a powerful ally. Asking critical questions as you turn over your inner soil often leads to new perspectives. Consider these:

What if you are a diamond just waiting to be discovered?

What if the belief that we are coal that needs to be mined to become a diamond is incorrect?

What if our work is not "figuring it out" but rather, awakening our awareness to the reality of what is?

Can you see that you are a gem?

Questions followed by reflection often support the expansion of our awareness to know the truth. Dedicate some time and distraction-free space to explore these prompts. It's a good idea to take these exercises in order. Each one builds upon the last, and as you gain confidence in your skills you'll be able to probe deeper with satisfying results. Have your journal with you to take some notes after each session. Feel free to record these reflections in your own voice in advance, so that you can bring your full awareness to the experience. Experiment playfully as you give yourself a chance to consider another possibility. No matter what, please be patient with yourself as you proceed into this new terrain.

Let's re-center ourselves in our purpose; it will keep us on track. The purpose of this book is to empower you to grow in awareness, experience and expression of your Soul's Purposes—so that you can identify appropriate ways to manifest your ideals and highest potential in this lifetime. Your dreams and visions of fulfilling possibilities can be brought to life supported by insight, guidance, wisdom and compassion of your Soul. We know that this lifetime is infused with magnificent destiny, and you are here to enjoy all the blessings life has for you!

Through these exercises, we can give shape and form to our Soul-level truths, as we strategically prepare to experience and express our spiritual nature and purpose in life. It turns out that our long-sought personal fulfillment is a real blessing to the world, which needs us to share our unique gifts.

Prepare to explore the nature of the Soul, to examine the fascinating relationship between your inner reality and outer expression. Learn how to identify your Soul's Purposes, clear away obstructions to well-deserved satisfaction and success. Discover optimal, practical ways to make inspired choices, and move forward in life. Particularly empowering is understanding our co-creative connection with Source, and how our most cherished dreams are related to the entire human family.

Exercise: Ignite the Light

Open your Records following the protocol. Give yourself a minute to settle into the space.

Close your eyes and open your awareness. Bring yourself and all your attention to this place, at this time. Thoughts about other things in your life can be set aside. Concerns about the future can also wait. Let yourself be here, in this room, in your seat, here and now. This moment is good enough, without adding anything to it. In this very moment, all of life exists—within and around you. At this time, you are sitting in the fullness of life, as the fullness of life. You are here in co-creative partnership with the Divine.

Now, direct your attention to the space between the heart of the earth and your body. Here we find, see or sense, a beam of light emanating from the core of the planet directly to you, holding you up, supporting you on your journey. Open yourself to allow this ray of light to shine into and through you, right up through the center of your being, into your heart, continuing up into your head and out through your crown.

This beam of light continues on upward all the way through to the point of light approximately 18 inches above the crown of your head. You know this place. It is the region where your Soul becomes distinct, individualized as you. This is the realm of the collective, unified universal Soul, of which you are an essential part. It's a paradox and a mystery. You are a part of the whole and, at the same time, complete within yourself.

Here, at this level, we encounter a horizon of light that is breathtakingly beautiful. Peering up over this horizon, we detect—maybe visually, audibly or by sensing it—that light is streaming toward us from all directions, in front, behind on both sides and above. There is light moving toward us from places near and familiar, and also from places that are far, foreign and yet to be discovered. This is the light of life, your constant companion. It has been with you since the inception of your Soul, leading, shining the way ahead, traveling alongside you as your companion and even following behind you.

Now, return your attention to the column of light, at the center of your human self—go back into your body, through your crown, and into the cave of your heart. This is the intersecting zone of the light from the earth and the light from the heavens. As you move into your heart space, the light from above follows, streaming into you, flooding your entire being, saturating every molecule, every atom of your being, mixing with the already present light energies of the earth. Expand your awareness to grasp yourself as the region where heaven and earth find harmony with you, a dynamic, loving, co-creative relationship through you, the human being. The finest, highest qualities and characteristics of spiritual truth are established in you, and expressed through you. You are a focal point of receptivity for the heavens and earth, almost like a satellite dish receiving and radiating love to everyone you encounter.

Now, expand your sense of yourself from head to toe while staying within your heart space. At this time, allow the infinite, unlimited, eternal, magnificent light within you to shine out through who you are as a person, in front, behind and on both sides. Consider the light going in front of you. Watch/sense as it travels out, through and beyond you into your life, your community, country, continent, following the natural curve of the earth, shining without effort. And from behind, the same light is shining through you, your world, your community out over the globe extending all the way around. Sense the light shining out through your sides as it follows the same pattern through you, into your life, and beyond, like arms of light wrapping around the world to give it a hug. And here you sit, with the light pouring through your crown, filling you up, radiating 360 degrees, wrapping itself around the world and all its inhabitants.

Once you've embraced the entire planet in light and love, open your awareness another step. Let yourself become aware of the light of others. See how it is supportive, complimentary to your own. As your light extends around the earth, you meet with others, similar in consciousness and shared intentions, with love and dedication to the well-being and enhancement of humanity. We are lovers of people, lovers of life. Here we make connections with likeminded souls, some we know, others we will never meet in this lifetime. Our lights combine, constituting a grid of light, a weave of layers of light, penetrating darkness, coldness and ancient fears, liberating ourselves and others from limiting patterns. No special action is required. We simply allow the light to find its way through us, and it is infinitely satisfying. So, here we stand, as points of light within a greater field of light that would cease to exist without our contributions.

For now, return your attention to the room where you're sitting. At this moment there are others like yourself, consciously directing their attention to the reality of the light, some nearby, others spanning continents, all joined in consciousness. We find ourselves in the company of others like ourselves—everyone present as a result of a deep inner prompting of Soul—with deep dedication to knowing and living the highest truths, expressing infinite love.

Now, in this place, open your awareness to yourself as a pillar of light within a field of light. Extend this light to the walls, front and back, both sides, consciously filling the room with light perfectly calibrated to who you are and what you need. And we reside in an optimal field of light, supporting us, empowering us on this amazing adventure!

Close your Records.

After the Exercise

Once we are centered in the reality of the light, we can begin to explore deeper. It can be helpful to make notes as you progress, to track your ever- expanding awareness. The process of writing helps honor the truths we are recognizing, no matter how obvious they seem. Validating our experiences through journaling is a powerful way to nurture our growth. With a sense of the presence of the light, let's move now to activate our awareness of the Soul's blueprint. We want to notice the nature of light itself and our standard, human responses to our experiences of the light.

Every time we visit our Records we go further into the richness. We become accustomed to this realm and discover best practices for engaging here. If you're in a hurry, this will stall your inevitable progress. This is a good time to take a deep breath, settle into your process and get ready for another deeper dive.

You are now ready to look more closely at the nature of your Soul, which will illuminate the elements of your path and purposes as outlined in the vibrational blueprint woven into the fabric of your Soul.

8

Your Soul's Blueprint

What is Soul?

Soul is the primary element within all living beings. Even though invisible to the human eye, Soul is the life force present in every atom of the Universe; it comprises the context and consciousness of life itself. We are each unique, personal expressions of one unified Soul, whose nature is spiritual, and essence is love. And within each of us is an infinite, eternal reservoir of love awaiting our conscious connection.

Soul is incorruptible. Nothing we do, or fail to do, can harm Soul. Inextricably fused into the fabric of our being, Soul cannot be stolen, damaged, diminished or given away; it's energetically impossible to destroy. Soul holds all of the wisdom and compassion cultivated over incarnations. There is no such thing as a dark or evil soul. It is always good. Actually, there is nothing we can do to diminish the light of the Soul—our own, or others. And, nothing can be done to us to extinguish the light of our soul. Soul is our inner Divine spark, reflecting our Divine presence.

When thinking about the relationship between Soul and the Divine, consider the natural connection between the moon as it reflects the light of the sun. Soul is a reflective realm, like a mirror or a lake, reflecting Divine essence out into the world. Each individual Soul is a fundamental component of Universal Soul, a dimension of consciousness fully aware of its Divine nature, which is both reflective and expressive of ultimate essence, each fragment containing the wholeness of Ultimate Reality. Since the purpose of Universal Soul is unconditional love for all of creation, the purpose of each individual Soul is to consciously learn to effectively experience, express and enjoy unconditional love in its own unique, individual way through who we are, and where we find ourselves. While Love is infinite and eternal, it needs avenues for expression. So, as individual human beings, our Soul's Purpose is to love ourselves no matter what, and to effectively express that unconditional love in the world.

A Great Challenge/Opportunity

Herein lies our great spiritual challenge/opportunity: How can we be spiritually awake and also effectively engage in the world? Indeed, this is a significant challenge for our infinite inner beings to find harmony and fulfillment by self-expressing in the finite circumstances of our human form. And it is also our spiritual opportunity to discover what activates the infinite love within us, and to engage in activities that promote our experience of this limitless love. Our work is about unleashing infinite love for our own benefit, and blessing everyone we encounter. The compelling power of our Soul's Purposes is so fiercely inherent in our being that we are continuously seeking until we actualize our deep, inner longings. Especially when they may not make sense, even when others ridicule us, nothing can satisfy the Divine seeking expression and fulfillment through us— except our Soul's Purposes. And, yes, our Souls have more than one purpose.

A Spiritual Journey

Since the nature of Soul is spiritual, it follows that Soul's Purposes are also spiritual. Identifying Soul's Purposes requires a spiritual journey. Our spiritual journey involves establishing a sustainable connection with our Souls while remaining in alignment with our personal talents, gifts and abilities—so that the infinite love within us can move through us, as us. We are fortunate that who we are is optimal for successfully transmitting the love we hold. In this process of manifestation, who we are transforms Divine potential into expressions and experiences of love, all according to our Soul's blueprint. The blueprint holds the key to your authentic desires in this life and, interchangeably, your true dreams, hopes and wishes are the elements of your blueprint. With every glimpse or hint of what you want, you gather information about your potential, and the promises life holds for you this time around. Manifestation requires desire from the depths of our being, the core fabric of who we are, and these are the building blocks of Inspired Manifesting.

Embedded in the Soul of every human being lies all the treasures of awareness accumulated through lifetimes of experiences—and they are yearning for expression (i.e. our Inspired Manifesting). What's necessary for life here and now as me?

Our ordinary desires and interests are important clues in recognizing our Soul's Purposes. Our Soul's blueprint determines the unique role that we are here to play. This blueprint is not literal. We never see with our ordinary or even inner eye a map or actual blueprint. Rather, we are referring to the very individual combination of raw material in the form of gifts, talents and abilities outlining our unique human possibilities and probabilities to be manifested throughout our lifetimes. You are your Soul's first and best choice for expressing its purposes in this lifetime. You are not here to manifest anyone else's Soul's Purpose—not your mother's unlived dream, nor your spouse's deepest desire.

What is an Example of a Soul's Purpose?

Your Soul's Purposes may be expressed at work, but they need not fit into a job description or receive a paycheck. In fact, when people mistake "making a million dollars" or attaining a material goal for their purpose, it's fascinating to watch their energy shift once they satisfy it. It's worth restating: Manifesting Soul's Purposes is not measured by making money. I have seen people express their Soul's Purposes in many ways in the world of business, whether driving trucks, selling cigars, or serving as a security guard at a college parking garage, and I have also known clients whose purpose is to empower others (anyone they support is wildly successful). Motherhood and caretaking our elders are wonderfully worthy Soul's Purposes, despite not being included in the GDP. In all cases,Life rewards us with abundance when we experience and express unconditional self-love in the world.

As we manifest our Soul's Purposes as human beings in the world, we assume physical form on this plane of existence. Expression of our Divine potential involves co-creating with the Divine. Interestingly, certain experiences are available only to specific genders, races, religions, socio-economic status and so on, each providing a unique opportunity to manifest. How we uniquely experience and express love at this point in time is spirituality in action. In some lifetimes, we are here to learn how to love ourselves in poverty, at other times, in opulence. We encounter every variation of experience with regard to money. The financial arena is a wonderful laboratory for activating our inner spiritual awareness. By converting spiritual essence into physical experience and expression, we find our Soul's Purposes within our regular human selves. The resulting experience is feeling happy, fulfilled and useful.

A Word About Karma

Finally, we often toss around the term "karma" when it comes to hardships, implying that we must have done something terrible in a prior incarnation to warrant our current struggles. I want to suggest that karma, or the Law of Cause and Effect, is in play only when we have outstanding negative judgments. Critical assessments of ourselves, others and attending circumstances trigger repetition of the pattern until we make peace, or simply accept and allow situations and people to be exactly as they are. When we accept, the cause and effect cycle resumes. Throughout our incarnations, we are charged with making peace with all expressions of life, those comfortable as well as those distressing. Resolving karma requires relinquishing judgments to facilitate increasing spiritual awareness and bring Soul's Purposes to life. Now seems like the perfect time to reflect on all of this. Let's pause and consider the atmosphere of spiritual light, which is always present whether we notice or not. As it turns out, the greater our focus and awareness of this light, the more powerful it becomes for us as we learn from spiritual laws. This one being, that the object of our attention is always fortified for us by our awareness. Let's direct our attention to the truth of light, empowering our relationship with it.

Exercise: Spiritual Light Atmosphere

Open your Records using the Pathway Prayer Process©. Take a moment to settle into the space. Close your eyes and open your awareness. Let yourself settle into the sacred space of infinite, inner light—not your memory of the light, or your thoughts about the light, but the light as you glimpse it today. Spiritual light emanates its own atmosphere. Due to its essential nature, love is all pervasive, dominant and obvious. In the space of love, there's no room for fear and other disturbing qualities. Make note of the traits and characteristics you find—anything from tranquility to appreciation to enthusiasm—all are attributes of love.

As you describe the environment in which you find yourself, turn your attention to yourself. Consider how you are feeling in this realm. What emotions are stimulated as you sit in this sacred space? Scan yourself, looking to see if you get a sense of being surrounded by light/love, or if it's within. In truth, it lives in both places, but it can take a bit of practice to glimpse the reality of it. As you rest in this light, allow your vision to be elevated to the level of flawless love, compassion and understanding. Maybe you imagine putting on a pair of spiritual glasses that automatically correct your vision to see only the best of you, what's good, loving and true. Observing yourself from this perspective, see if you can identify some of the ways that you personally experience and express love in this life.

This is a good time to begin probing our inner world for insight into our Soul's Purposes. Maybe you can grasp a general sense of your Soul's Purposes and your destiny in this lifetime. Remember, your Soul's Purposes are directly related to experiences that unleash the infinite love within you. They are inherently spiritual. Don't worry about the details, this is a process, not a one-time event. If you believe in reincarnation—that your Soul is on a journey through countless human identities to awaken to the spiritual truth of who you are—perhaps you can get a sense of how this particular life fits within the scheme of all your lifetimes.

While you are in this reflective state, you can consider what is distinct or impressive about your Soul's Purposes in this life. It's possible you'll have a sense of some realistic yet inspiring possibilities for you in this life. Take your time. Know that you can always return to these rich inner spaces where all the truth of you is waiting to be discovered. When you are ready, open your eyes and return your attention to the room.

Close your Records using the Prayer, and let yourself return to your ordinary state of mind.

Reflection: Pillar of Light

In this next exercise, we have a chance to cultivate the connection between our inner light, and the world in which we live. Before we dive in, there are a few ideas that will help you negotiate this inner space. From the angle of spiritual truth, the core of our being is infinite, eternal light. At the center of our being is a pillar of light rooted at the base of our body, extending up through the trunk and out the top of the head. This central pillar holds the chakras or energy vortexes in place. Composed of grace, an elegant expression of unconditional love, it is a wonderful place from which we can examine our relationship with life.

It can be helpful to think of this central pillar of light as our own personal sanctuary, a space of reverence committed to us personally for our inner explorations and discoveries of resident truth and wisdom. Since it is ours, we are always welcome to visit and even dwell for our encouragement and restoration, here in the home of pure light and love.

Exercise: Refreshing the Links from Your Inner Light to Your Outer Life: The Five Pillars

Again, take your time and open your Akashic Records, following the instructions and thoughtfully considering the words as you read them.

Begin by directing your attention to the pillar of light at the center of your being, starting at the base of your spine, your root chakra, moving up through the trunk of your body, and out through the crown chakra. Find a place within the pillar to center yourself. Sit within the pillar and look out beyond it, through yourself out into the world. Direct your gaze forward.

See if you can recognize a pillar of light directly in front of you, but still within your body. You may have a visual impression of this pillar or simply sense something existing in this place. This is the pillar of Incarnation. Take a moment to review your relationship with the particulars of this lifetime. Making peace with who we are as human beings and the ordinary realities of our lives is the first step in our transformation. What problems have you/your family wrestled with? What if who you are as a person is ideal for the demonstration and expression of your Soul's Purposes? What if the person that you are is your Soul's first and best choice in this lifetime?

Now, move your awareness to the front right side of your body, to the pillar of Authority. Reflect on your general relationship with Authority. As long as we are here on earth, we find ourselves connected to authorities. Finding our place and peace with authority is an imperative of the human experience. Do you tend to reject or judge authority? Are you normally fearful of authority? Notice your standard response to authority. Are you willing to allow imperfect authority figures like your parents to transmit the perfect energy of authority to you?

Redirect your awareness to the right side of your back body, looking out to the pillar of Discipline. With discipline, we establish pathways through which the power of life flows to and from us. What is your automatic reaction to the idea of discipline? Do you reject it? Do you confuse punishment with discipline? Are you more prone to over-discipline or under-discipline yourself? Is there a pattern of behavior that would quiet your mind and empower you to hear the inner voice of truth?

Next, focus on the left side of your back body, looking out to the pillar of Responsibility. Make note of your general response. Responsibility is the crucible within which we transform into our best selves. Observe your patterns of true and/or false responsibilities in this lifetime. True responsibilities refine us into our optimal selves; false responsibilities deplete us. Consider your level of willingness to be transformed by your true responsibilities in this life.

At this point, let your awareness travel to the left side of your front body, gazing out to the fifth pillar of light, Commitment. This is a remarkable quality, adhering us to our values as we navigate the stormy waters of life and unleashing the promises embedded in our path. Notice your "go-to" or default. Do you avoid commitment? Or do you become engulfed by it? Is there a commitment you can embrace at this time in your life that will activate the power of your path? Remember, your path can only nurture you once you commit.

Now, bring your awareness back into the central pillar of light, the pillar of Grace and find a place to rest. Grace is spacious, yet intimate, safe but encouraging. A perfect fit, grace provides precise support for us and our needs at any given moment. The sensitivity of Grace is practically heartbreaking in its beauty and splendor—and, here it is, within us, for us. Observe the clarity of the pillars, notice how the infinite light at the center of your shining out through you into the world. There is no need to send light, simply allow it to find its way through and beyond you as it radiates. At the same time, the light magnetizes what you need to bring your Soul's Purposes to life. Stand as a lighthouse, so you can be easily recognized by everything seeking you.

In the fullness of this experience, close your Records using the Pathway Prayer Process©. Give yourself a chance to reconnect to your day.

After the Exercises

Wonderful! These exercises can reveal quite a bit, so I recommend you ease back into your day. Drink some water, take a slow walk around the block. Note any insights. After you center yourself, we will be ready to move on and shift gears to learn how to recognize your Soul's Purposes.

You've had a chance to clarify the relationship between your Inner Light and Truth and the way you engage in the world. We know you are committed to aligning your inner awareness to aspects of the ordinary world and this is a great way to bridge those pieces. Doing this exercise gives you a chance to upgrade, or update your relationship between your inner truth and the outer world. If you do this periodically, you can stay current so that the light at the core of your being flows easily into the world and, at the same time, the blessings of the world can find their way directly into your heart. Now that we've had a chance to strengthen Soul's Purposes.

9

Top 10 Clues You are
Living Your Soul's Purpose

So, how do you know your Soul's Purposes? Any one of these
clues may provide insight to affirm or clarify your Soul's Purposes.

1. You want to do what has to be done to realize your goal.
Your ordinary desires and interests are a very important clue. If
it's your Soul's Purpose, your desire is evident. Even when you
don't understand and aren't certain, you read about it, talk about
it, experiment, and investigate. If you have zero interest, it is simply not yours to do. The Universe will not give you a purpose
that you dread. So, let's consider what connects us with our inner desires: "What gives me energy today? What activates the energy within me? What amplifies that?" Our Soul's Purposes are
designed to bring us much closer to loving, enjoying, and appreciating who we are. Actually, they take us into true intimacy with
ourselves.

**2. You have some natural ability, and are able to do what
needs to be done with what you have.** While pursuing your Soul's

Purposes may not be convenient or comfortable, you can do what is needed to complete the next step. I can remember a time decades ago when I was experimenting with my own work. During the day I was cleaning houses and, at night, I was giving tarot readings. Without a car, I had only my bike and went from shop to shop hanging my flyers. I was satisfied, and also had a sense that there was more for me. Given who I am and what I have, what can I do? Keep asking the question, and life will keep expanding the answer.

3. **You actually enjoy the process, even when it's difficult or demanding.** It's a myth that our purpose comes easy and requires no effort. In fact, sometimes there's bad weather and lots of traffic, and it feels really hard. Even though our Soul's Purposes require discipline, responsibility and commitment, they can be quite enjoyable, and unleash inner happiness. Soul Purposes are designed to bring us closer to appreciating who we are. As I watch my partner make pottery, I see how infinitely satisfying the creative process is. When I am consumed with one of my projects, no invitation no matter how fun can distract me or entice me away from my work. People may not understand how compelling this is for you. I love to ice skate. One day I remember watching a young boy just skate and skate around the rink. No matter what his dad tried, he couldn't get him off the ice.

4. **You have enough energy and resources to take the very next step.** You are willing to learn and develop yourself to expand your skills to achieve the object of your purpose. Timing is important as well. Ten years ago I didn't have the energy or resources for a new website. Today I do. I have enough energy and resources and knew to ask for lots of assistance from the experts to execute. Life makes sure we have what we need to complete our Soul's Purposes.

5. **You are clear about the experience of your destination, and flexible about how it all comes to fruition.** You know how it feels to be fulfilled and satisfied, enriched and free. While you may be

fixed on the experience of the destination, you are also flexible about the path for getting there and open to changes along the way. You understand that life is your laboratory.

6. Perfection is not required. You don't wait for the perfect circumstances or for developing your perfect character. You begin. And when you encounter obstacles, you find ways to work around them. No matter the challenge, you find a way to be at peace with yourself as you navigate your way through. You stay the course. Quitting is not an option.

7. Your work has value in and of itself, whether or not others support you, approve of it, value it or tell you that it matters. You may enjoy, but do not need the support or approval of others. You recognize that you can't do it alone, you learn how to find appropriate support, you are willing to ask for and receive assistance.

8. You trust that there's something greater at work—life. I remember being confused about this, thinking I had to learn to trust other people but found myself often disappointed. Of course, I did. We are all imperfect beings each traveling our own path. When I am aware of my relationship with life and have a sense that "This is mine to do," I find the support that is expressive of the value I place on my purpose. I can recall standing in a bookstore years ago, hungrily seeking. Then it came to me: I would have to write the book I wanted to read!

9. You begin where you are, with what you have, accept assistance as needed and continue alone if necessary with no attachment to how much time, effort or resources are required.

10. You love yourself, no matter the outcome. You know that you are an important piece of the connected whole and that, without your contribution, everything would be different. You completely love and accept yourself and know that your Soul's Purposes are yours to do.

These simple guidelines can be a big help when trying to identify or sort out our Soul's Purposes. Many people report that their purposes are "no big deal," which is why they didn't consider them valuable. Our Soul's Purposes are a natural part of who we are! They are built into our personalities and character, as well as our fondest dreams for ourselves. Most striking about our Soul's Purposes is that they persist in the face of opposition. We have the talent to realize them and, when we move in their direction, they self-generate. The more we grow into them by taking action, the greater our desire and motivation to continue. Born from a place of spiritual purity in our Soul, these purposes stimulate our experience of being loved, loving and lovable all at the same time. And, this crucible of love births our dreams into reality, giving us the Inspired Manifesting we came to life to experience.

Radiate Light, Magnetize Good

The nature of light is equally radiant and magnetic. As our obstructions dissolve, the light at the core of our being radiates out through us into the world. This beam is a unique, individual expression of the Divine through us that travels through and infinitely beyond us. At the same time, the light, by its magnetic nature, is naturally drawing to us everything we need to support our Soul's journey in this life. Due to our individualized expressions, we will only and always attract exactly what resonates with our frequency of light. Anything unrelated will be undesirable, and impossible to attract. As we expand our range of expression and attraction, the obstructions to our radiance diminish, the light within us lets those who are seeking us know we are available.

We are always fully satisfied by what is ours, and never fulfilled by what is not ours. There is never enough of what we don't want and always more than enough of what we really desire. Begin by considering the eternal truth of existence—your essential nature. You may see it in a pillar of light or sense it energetically within. As you practice seeing the infinite light and love that is the core of your being, your ability to recognize and radiate light, and magnetize good quickens. Consciously radiating light and magnetizing good is the primary light dynamic for Inspired Manifesting.

Spiritual Fitness

Over the years, I have met many spiritual seekers dedicated to improving the quality of their lives, sincerely striving to manifest love and wisdom. A question they often ask is, "How can I become the highest spiritual version of myself?" Curiously, it turns out that in this co-creative process with the Divine Reality, our part is to condition our human self to be of maximum usefulness. This involves paying attention to our bodies, emotions, minds and doing our best to take good care of ourselves.

When we are compromised because we are physically neglected, suffering emotional distress or mental confusion, our ability to identify light/love, harness these qualities and express them is sorely limited—not impossible, but thwarted. Our fitness is fundamental to our ability to manifest satisfaction and success. In this next exercise, we have a chance to reflect on our overall well-being, as well as request support for our improvement. Think back to the idea of the chalice. When the stem is solid, the platform secure, the cup can hold the finest wine without threat of spilling. It's the same with us, and accommodating light/love.

Exercise: Spiritual Fitness Practice

Open your Records following the instructions. Give yourself a chance to acclimate to the Akashic Atmosphere, characterized by warmth, acceptance and appreciation. It normally responds to our needs at any given time, and the dominant, discernible qualities of love modify to best serve us.

Take a few moments to find your personal center. Notice what qualities of love are especially strong today. Is it safety and security?

Or appreciation and enthusiasm? Endless expressions of love come to us in ways we need on any given day. Pay attention to the combination of qualities expressing love to you today. Directing your attention inward, How are you doing today? Perhaps you feel some worry or are experiencing a few body aches. It's completely normal to have a combination of conditions occurring at the same time within you. Make note of what they are. Be as specific as possible.

Now, focus on your body. How is your body doing today? You may be full of energy, or depleted. What's important is that you become more aware of the quality of your health. Can you glean insight into any health concerns you may have?

Next, consider your emotions or feelings. How are you feeling today? Are you happy? Sad? Anxious? Excited? Or some other combination of feelings? Pay attention to the blend of emotions you have today. Maybe you are serene with a bit of worry about something. Don't try to change what you feel; all of your feelings are valuable. It's more helpful to identify and name your emotions. Can you make peace with all the emotions you have today? If there is a particular feeling that's uncomfortable for you, ask for help resolving that emotion.

Turn your attention to your thoughts. Notice what you are thinking about and the type of thoughts you generally have. You may be entertaining thoughts of something wonderful, someone you love perhaps, or quite possibly the ideas going through your mind are negative. It's also possible you are reviewing your fears and making yourself unnecessarily fearful.

We always have the power of choice when it comes to our thoughts. We humans have the great privilege of selecting our own thoughts. So, if the ideas in your mind are disturbing to you, stop thinking about them, and start thinking about something that makes you happy. If you are having difficulty changing your thoughts, ask your spiritual support team for guidance. You are entitled to feel peace and well-being. You can help yourself by deliberately thinking about things that are pleasing to you.

Let's consider the day ahead, just this day. The past is over and the future is not here yet, so let's think about today. Review your plans for the day. What do you expect to experience, what do you hope to accomplish, who do you want to meet, and what other activities are on your calendar? It's very likely that there are some things you are looking forward to and others you wish you didn't have to do! How can you be more empowered to deal with your day, all the activities and people, with love and respect?

Take the insight, guidance and wisdom provided into your heart. And close your Records.

After the Exercise

Excellent. Now, turn your attention to this moment. Notice that you are fully alive, no matter what flaws and ready to move forward to the best of your ability. Know that your best will be good enough and enjoy!

By now, you are warmed up enough to take another step toward grasping your Soul's Purposes. I like to think of myself standing at the shore of one of the world's great oceans. While the entire ocean is present and welcoming, I have to wade in, one little step at a time. This approach is particularly helpful when the magnificence of the resource can be overwhelming. It's wise to give yourself the time and space to discover a beneficial pace. There's no race, no competition. We're all guaranteed success at our own ideal time. So take good care of yourself along the way. Our next exercise is to probe the question of our Soul's Purposes.

Exercise: Exploring Soul's Purposes in the Zone of Choice

Open your Records using the Pathway Prayer Process©. Take a few moments to encounter the Akashic Atmosphere and to be embraced by it. Reconnect with your Masters, Teachers and Loved Ones—your dedicated spiritual support team. Let yourself be assisted in this process.

Now let's explore your experience with your own Soul. Is it inspiring, exciting, enthusiastic, or some combination? To the best of your ability, identify, describe and name these characteristics. What are some of the qualities you recognize as currently active in your Soul? How does this make you feel about yourself? Your life? The big picture of this life?

Now, let's go deeper. If you are working in your Akashic Records, ask to be guided into the Zone of Choice, that inner Akashic Realm we visit in between incarnations to evaluate our development and make selections for an upcoming lifetime. The Zone of Choice is an inner Akashic Realm, a dimension we visit in- between lifetimes to make choices for our upcoming lifetime. We make these selections in co-creative partnership with the Divine, supported by our Masters, Teachers and Loved Ones. Due to the exceptional scope and purity of this Realm, we can more easily recognize the wisdom of choices made along the way. Clarifying questions about such matters—our decision to be the person we are, why we opted for the family we belong to, and some of the particulars of this segment of our Soul's path—may provide insight into the promise of our Soul's Purposes.

This is not a destination for a casual visit and it can be uncomfortable at times. It is for those of us who are sincere and eager to take responsibility for our choices. Ask to reconnect to the space and time when your Soul, in partnership with the Divine, selected you as the ideal individual to bring your Soul's Purposes to life at this time. (Remember, you don't really "go" anywhere. This reconnection is an act of awareness.) At that time, you had some intentions, goals, aims, and objectives for yourself in this incarnation. Can you identify them? Keep in mind that the Soul is spiritual, so the intentions will be related to love in both general and specific ways.

You also had some expectations. Let's examine those. How did you think this life would unfold? What did you expect? What seemed likely to happen? Now, focus on your actual experience of living this life. Over the course of this incarnation, you have had many moments when you were flooded with awareness and sensations of love. The unlimited love within you was activated or encouraged. You felt it as emotion, and it poured through you out into your life. Notice what conditions, circumstances even thoughts initiated that experience of love awakening within you. Ask to recognize those powerful times when the love within you rose up and poured through you.

Now, let's direct our attention to this time in your life. What circumstances stimulate your awareness of the love within you? Given the current state of your resources, what action can you take to ignite the flow of love? What can you do in the next 24 hours to experience, express and enjoy the love within?

Now, let's move back into the Akasha at large. Simply retrace your steps to return. Take a moment here to review your intentions, expectations, experiences of love. Finally, identify the point of power, engaging your will, the point through which the Soul's Purposes become tangible here on earth, noticing what you can actually do to activate even more love than ever before, right here and now, just the way you are. Say the Closing Prayer and let yourself fully return your awareness to this day.

After the Exercise

When you make notes about the exercise we just did, describe as much as possible without trying to evaluate everything immediately. Venturing into the Zone of Choice can stir up a new level of awareness and sometimes it takes more grounding to completely return. Known as extremely potent for clarifying our personal responsibility, why we made certain choices and the positive value of the decisions we've made in our lives. Remember, you can return at any time. This is your process, these are your Records, this is your Soul and your truth. You are the boss. If you feel the need to return to the Zone of Choice please do, and give yourself the gift of inner spiritual awareness.

We've spent some time now unearthing the truth about the

valid, wise choices we made when we selected the circumstances of this lifetime. Your co- creative connection with the Divine has always been operational. You have some tools to help you identify your Soul's Purposes, and understand more about the relationship between your human self and your Soul's Purposes. With our foray into the Zone of Choice, you are demonstrating courage and a willingness to take responsibility for your choices. You also have a good sense of the gap between your expectations and the reality of your life as it unfolds. This is quite a slice of reality, and you are downright heroic for diving in. Our landscapes are taking shape, our foundations are solid, now we move onto the magnificent manifestation process.

IO

The Magnificent Process of Manifesting

The word manifesting literally means: to make obvious, to demonstrate, to bring about in physical form. Inspired Manifestation occurs through us when our desires, talents, and skills converge with our taking action in the world. We are always manifesting—this is our natural relationship to life. We simply can't not manifest. Even when we call a halt to all activities and sit down on the couch, this is still a form of manifesting. Something is always emanating from us, whether comfortable or not, favorable or not, conscious or not. The nature of our personal evolution is manifesting. When we manifest, we make evident something that has been inspired through us by the Divine. By honoring natural laws, we make our ideas real in time and space, here on earth (as opposed to magic, which is done by supernatural forces working outside of natural laws).

Manifesting happens within the life we are living, through the human beings we are, and in the place where our personal dreams intersect with the world. In the crosscurrent of our individual selves with the greater world, our Soul's Purposes take form—they manifest.

While we are ultimately capable of anything and everything across all incarnations, this is where we make decisions about our strengths and weaknesses for this lifetime. While manifesting is done unconsciously at first, with increasing awareness, we begin to perform conscious, deliberate, preferred manifesting.

Manifesting calls us onto a path of exploration, motivated by our search to discover the truth. Manifesting is the inevitable outcome of our spiritual being in action in our material world. Who we are is the ideal convergence zone between spiritual and material worlds, between universal purpose and individual intention, between Universal Soul's Purposes and Soul's Purposes. By manifesting our Soul's Purposes, the eternal fusion of our humanity and spiritual core is revealed, empowering us to experience life beyond perceived dualities: in a multi-dimensional reality of oneness.

A Paradox Arises

How does our infinite inner being find harmony and fulfillment self-expressing in the restricted circumstances of our finite human form? By expanding our spiritual awareness and taking action in the world we co-create with the Divine. Manifesting our Destiny requires time + space + matter and is the result of three converging dimensions: human being (who we are) + Soul (spiritual core reflecting Divinity) + in the world (as is, right now).

Manifesting our Destiny requires time + space + matter. It is the result of three converging dimensions: human being (who we are) + Soul (spiritual core reflecting Divinity) + in the world (as is, right now).

In the big picture, humanity is right now experiencing a massive evolutionary upgrade, a fundamental shift in consciousness. For ages, we have lived within dualistic thinking: right/wrong, good/bad, black/white, heaven/hell. These aren't terrible ideas, but we have gone as far as we can go with them. Actually, they reflect the highest interpretation we humans have had about the nature of life and all its participants. Emerging from dualistic consciousness, our challenge and opportunity are to shift into oneness—unitary consciousness. The difficulty in this task is that it requires being reasonably comfortable with paradox, something our rational, dualistically conditioned minds find troublesome, if not impossible.

A paradox is a seeming contradiction: something that seems to be absurd, but is actually true. You may recall my discussion about this earlier. I'm an infinite being, and I'm a finite being. I'm perfect; I'm imperfect. I'm unlimited, and I'm limited. These pairs are all true at the same time, but only when viewed at different levels. At the Soul-level, I am infinite. At the human level, I am finite. At the Soul- level, I am perfect. At the human level, I am imperfect. At the Soul-level, I am unlimited. At the human level, I am limited. The truth is that we are complex human beings living in a multi-dimensional world; we naturally contain many paradoxes. The challenge is to embrace both parts of the duality; without choosing one, let both be true. Fortunately, we already have this capacity as there is spaciousness within the human heart to house paradox.

Struggling to reconcile paradoxes is like fighting a losing battle. In the days of dualism—believing in two powers (good and bad, right and wrong)—it made sense to try to find a middle ground, or to eliminate one of the components of the paradox. But, in this age of Oneness, everything is included. There is ample room for acceptance of all pairs of opposites. We do not have to cancel one out over the other. This inclusivity fosters continually expanding expressions. And, in fact, Inspired Manifesting requires open space, a judgment-free, restriction-free arena for experimentation and growth. Liberated from prior limitations, we are free to attempt—to fail and succeed—in short, to learn. Inclusivity implies safety, which is a necessary ingredient for Inspired Manifesting.

Opening to paradox, we begin to sense the reality of our individual human selves co-existing and interrelating within a sea of other interdependent beings, each and all of us requiring the presence of each other to manifest our Soul's Purposes. This realization offers a tremendous opportunity to relinquish negative judgments about ourselves and others and instead to acknowledge, accept and appreciate our natural connectedness.

Here's another paradox: Within the metaphor of this ocean of all beings— each of equal value and uniqueness in their own individual identity—no one of us is the same nor is any of us more special than another. And also, everyone is essential for the whole to be exactly as it is, just as every cell in the body—albeit different in form and function—is required for the body to function. Within the unified sea of interdependent beings, we each have a unique opportunity to manifest our individual selves. We are each and all vital for the whole of the Universe to thrive! (If at first you don't comprehend, feel free to re-read and reflect upon this truth.)

You can see that the spiritual practice of paradox serves a vital function in the manifestation process. It is quite useful for challenging old ideas embedded in the collective consciousness, and our personal twist on concepts such as duality and separation. Because paradox provides a useful cognitive construct for accommodating the post-2012 shift to oneness, it can help the human mind to accept contrary ideas. To be clear, I am not suggesting a stance of enlightened passivity, but rather encouraging a more visionary approach that will launch us into an expansion of awareness. We do not resolve paradoxes; we allow both concepts to exist simultaneously in a both/and way (instead of the dualistic either/or mindset which calls for either/or), such as I am both finite and infinite. Requiring courage, paradox ennobles the heart to manage the strain of mediating between the opposite orbs. Practicing the power of paradox challenges humans to let go of our mind's steady grasp on the truth, which opens the portal from duality to unity consciousness. One of the great gifts of this essential spiritual practice is this: the more comfortable we are with paradox, the more aliveness we can accommodate.

Empowering our ability to accommodate paradox is our ever-expanding sensitivity to the presence of the unseen power of life, the force or God, whatever term you like. As we grow into greater conscious awareness that there is a quality of life that is good, loving, kind, appreciative, enthusiastic and a million other expressions of love, we can relax. It becomes easier to surrender archaic notions based on fear and cryptic approaches to life founded on superstition. Recognizing loving attributes in endless form, our sense of emotional and physical safety is fortified. Expanding our sense of freedom, safety and trust in life we can make room within ourselves for paradoxes we encounter. There's no pressure to select one option over the other, or to ignore the existence of both. Simply find a greater space within to hold the paradox and restore inner peace—*Voila!*

Exercise: Making Peace with Paradox Begin by opening your Records

Bring your attention to the infinity symbol, the number 8 on its side. Notice how both orbs of the symbol are of equal weight, space, outline and value. Allow your awareness to travel on this symbol as you step in at the singular point in the center linking both orbs, and let yourself glide along to the right, tracing the line of the symbol all the way around and back to the center point. Now, glide along to the left side of the orb, tracing the line of the symbol all the way around and back to the center point. Perhaps you can get a sense of how much life force moves from one segment of the symbol to the other.

Now, in our effort to make peace with paradox, imagine placing one foot on one part of the symbol and the other foot on the other part of the symbol. It might feel like it's rocking or rolling, that's okay. Find a way to balance yourself in the presence of a living paradox, while the paradox remains unchanged. Settling into the field of infinite light, get a sense of being in the center point of the sphere that is you. In this space of eternal compassion and acceptance, let yourself register that this realm is a unified field composed of all of the energetic equivalents of life, both potential and realized or demonstrated aspects. Get a sense of the flow of life that is happening here: the exchange, the interconnectedness. So here you are getting some sense of balance with living with paradox, like being on a surfboard or skateboard. Scan your body and notice the fluid movements required by your body, your emotions, your thinking. You instinctively know how to stand in the presence of paradox. The flexibility and adaptability required are very natural to you.

As you engage this symbol, allow the paradox within to surface, identifying paradoxical ideas as they come to your mind, such as I am unlimited; I am limited. Moving back and forth, stand in the truth of that paradox or try another. I am everything; I am nothing. I am mortal; I am immortal. I am everything; I am nothing. I am infinite; I am finite. So for now, let this be. In your mind's eye, step off the infinity symbol back onto terra firma. Bring your attention back, and embrace the day!

Close your Akashic Records using the Protocol and make notes, describing your experience.

The Akashic Atmosphere

One of the essential elements for productive inner work is an atmosphere of non-judgment. It's perfect that the Akashic Records are governed by Three Absolutes, one of which is "Judge Not." This governing principle safeguards the space so we can tinker around to find the truths at any given time in our journey. We just saw the significance of emotional safety when considering paradox and the value of inclusion and unity in manifesting. There are even more ways "Judge Not" is beneficial as we engage this exploration. For example, tapping our imagination is another powerful segment of our journey, as it invites us to be more understanding and accepting of ourselves. The non-judgmental atmosphere of the Akasha is an ideal place to use our imagination, as it gives us emotional neutrality, along with space for exploration. We turn now to examine "imagination," learning its potential and role for our Inspired Manifesting.

Imagination

Sometimes, students worry that this is all just their imagination, and I wonder how the imagination got such a bad reputation. Imagination is an aspect of our inner reality, a treasury of possibility, dreams and hopes. There are those who say with certainty that the imagination of man is the sliver of God. That may be true. But, for our purposes, what's important is that each of us has our own, personal imagination. Were we all to gather and imagine an ideal day, there would be as many descriptions as individuals. No two of us have the exact imagination. But all imaginations share the same qualities of originality, visionary, inspirational, sensitivity, etc. I invite you to set aside your concerns about the validity of imagination, and open up to what could become for you.

Although quite different in form and function, there is a relationship between paradox and imagination. Paradox, as previously mentioned, is the existence of two seemingly antagonistic variables—ranging from ideas to events— which appear to contradict and cancel out one another. Actually, both are true but in different realms. Imagination is the aspect of our inner awareness that is imbued with all the raw materials necessary to conjure up unique options for expressing our most authentic impulses, in ways that nurture and sustain us.

Certainly you can discern the distinctions. But they emerge from a shared space, a judgment-free zone of acceptance and allowing. When these ingredients come together, they foster expanded horizons, open mindedness and curiosity, because of the emotional safety and lack of ridicule occupying the environment. Notice the positive consequences of acceptance. It's deceptive because it appears so simple and unassuming and, yet, this is the birthplace of possibility for human beings.

Spiritual Practices Take Time

As we continue, remember that engaging your inner reality using the Akashic Records is a spiritual practice that takes time. This is not fortune telling, where scant awareness is involved and "answers" are immediate. When working in the Records, our journey to expanding awareness is paramount. Appropriate understanding and expectations of yourself and the resource contribute to satisfying guidance and valuable wisdom. As you proceed, be especially kind to yourself. Know that it takes courage to be receptive to new learning, and you are in the midst of a daring adventure.

Give yourself the chance to observe and describe your experiences. Rushing to evaluate can impede our progress. Noticing and describing brings our experiences into focus and, in the long run helps us comprehend the ways they are contributing to our growth. Take your time to describe, as if you were sharing with a loyal friend, and as you put words to what "seems" to be, the nuggets of gold at the center of our awareness come into focus, and we begin to understand more than before.

It is the rare person who has a "one time" flash of their Soul's Purposes. And my hat's off to that one. But for most of us, this awareness is progressive: one notion at a time, one possibility, one glimmer of what could be, maybe. Added up over time, these come together to form a rich tapestry suggesting an image that seems so new and exciting, yet familiar. Our Soul's Purposes are not totally foreign to us, they live within. Our work is to awaken to the awareness of what already lives and that is seeking expression through us.

We are growing in our personal sensitivity to our inner truth, and the outer actions necessary to facilitate our growth. Let's turn our attention toward greater understanding of the nature of our inner spiritual power, as well as best ways to activate it and use it well. It's already present, so there's no need to try to generate it, but it remains dormant until we notice and interact with it. Let's bring our focus to this aspect of our journey.

Exercise: Your Spiritual Manifesting Power

Open your Records using the Pathway Prayer Process©. Be sure to read the Prayer rather than memorize it. This ensures the vitality of our connection. I know you deserve and desire a superior relationship with your own Soul and the Records. Keep your practice alive by reading the Prayer each time. It works!

Give yourself a chance to settle into the sacred space at the center of your being. It's perfectly acceptable to pretend or imagine this as real. Your imagination is a spiritual launching pad for your visions. Over the course of the past exercises, you have had some ideas or inclinations about your possible Soul's Purposes. They may not be fully developed, which is fine. We are working with the raw material of new ideas. Make note of what you think might be some of your Soul's Purposes in this lifetime.

Excellent. This is a very important incarnation for you. It is time for you to achieve remarkable growth and experience authentic, spiritual manifestation. You are here to bring your Soul's Purposes to life, and to enjoy the process. This is why you are committed to this process. The number one requirement for igniting your spiritual manifesting power is your personal happiness. Your happiness and well-being are critical and essential. Do your ideas make you happy? Are they satisfying? Fulfilling? Inspiring? Does the very thought of any of these possible purposes make you happy? Does the prospect of moving ahead with any of these ideas make you feel good about yourself?

Do they make you feel that you are "good enough"? Or not quite adequate?

Do these ideas seem a bit impossible for you? Or are they within your reach? Are you inspired by any of these options? Do they cause you to want to learn, examine, explore and experiment? Are you willing to take action on any of these even if you are not successful at the beginning? Are you willing to try any of these even if they fail?

Can you love yourself no matter what the outcome? Are you open to being deliberately kind and respectful to yourself if you are successful? How about if you stumble and fall? Are you open to adjusting your vision? Are you willing to use your good common sense to modify your purposes?

Say the Closing Prayer to close the Records.

After the Exercise

In order for your Inspired Manifestation to be powerful, you may have to make some adjustments. This is to be expected. Let yourself adjust your vision of your Soul's Purposes, and consider your revised ideal. This process can be repeated as often as necessary. Remember the #1 requirement is your personal happiness. You are doing so well. Keep your ideas close to your heart. If you are aching to share it with another, make sure they understand the importance of this mission, and respect your quest.

By now, you have a delicate embryo of your Soul's Purposes at this point in your life. Any inclination you have to protect it makes such good sense. Let's carry this precious awareness, full of promise in the depths of our being as we consider some of the nuts and bolts of demonstrating our truth as the people we are, living in the world, just the way it is. Basic understanding of how the process works will inform the optimal ways for us to proceed at this exquisitely sensitive yet explosively exciting juncture. We'll need to know what Manifesting is, how it works, the necessary ingredients in addition to how we can apply all of these to bring about an inspiring result! Take a deep breath and then join me in our next segment.

II

Manifesting Your Soul's Purposes

Manifestation occurs through us as human beings, right here in real time on earth. Note that manifestation happens through us, not to us. We manifest through our being human, not outside of our humanity. Manifesting our Soul's Purposes is a demonstration of the dynamic interrelationship between us as individual humans and life on earth. Manifestation occurs within the Realm of Engagement—that wonderful transformational crucible where life, the Divine spark, and our humanity (especially our Soul's Purposes and our Inner Triangle) meet. Let's look at how this process occurs.

Manifesting is not a singular event. We cannot do it alone, and it is not accomplished in a single moment in time. Instead, manifesting is a constantly changing process that takes place throughout our entire lifetime, as we engage and express love with each other within the context of the unified whole. While we are awakening, accepting, allowing, appreciating, and expressing love—with ever- increasing awareness, consciousness, responsibility and respect, our manifestation changes to reflect the unfolding of our personal understanding.

As we manifest, we demonstrate the life force at the core of our being, and our Soul's Purposes take form.

With this, we see manifesting as a dynamic relational engagement requiring our constant attention and awareness. We are all equal parts of one whole, each making our own worthy, needed contribution. Each person, place, and thing is related. Without every being that has ever existed, the Universe would not be what it is today. Recognizing our own unique value, and others', we appreciate that we are all individual expressions of life manifesting individually within one interconnected whole.

Love is Essential for Inspired Manifesting:
The Triangle Test

For manifestation to occur, an idea must inspire love, activate our experience of love, or encourage us to express love in meaningful and satisfying ways. Happiness and well-being are required for manifestation to occur. As multi- dimensional beings, we owe it to ourselves to consider the different aspects of our humanity. Any project, dream, or program we hope to bring to fruition will have to meet the Triangle Test: Heart, Mind and Will. Applying this requires asking these questions:

1. **HEART:** "Do I love this? Does the prospect of this possibility make me happy?" Am I excited or filled with dread? If the reality of doing the necessary work makes you want to cry, chances are good that the final result will not make you happy either. We cannot suffer our way into happiness; positive feelings must ensue. Sure, we have to expend effort, and we may even be inconvenienced. But when something is true at the level of heart, taking appropriate action—manifesting our Soul's Purposes—makes us happy.

2. MIND: "Is it a good idea for me at this time? Does it make good sense for me?" Consider whether or not your dream, plan, or project makes good sense. Soul's Purposes will not be manifested if they are foolish, ridiculous or senseless. They must be meaningful and useful for manifestation to occur. And they are required to be wise for us personally. The world is full of great ideas, but not each one is a good fit for us. We want to make sure that the option under consideration is appropriate for us at this time in our life.

3. WILL: "Am I willing to take action on this, to do what's needed?" The realm of our will is the intersecting point of our Souls with the world in which we live. With our will, we deliver our wisdom into the world. This is another simple "yes" or "no" question: Am I willing to ... put in the hours, learn new skills, etc.? A few days of failed commitment can bring honesty. And, of course, at other times we may underestimate our willingness only to find that, as we begin, our enthusiasm expands, and we are surprisingly more willing than originally thought.

In summary, consider **the Triangle Test:**

- *Do I love this?* **(Heart)**
- *Is it a good idea?* **(Mind)**
- *Am I willing to do what's needed?* **(Will)**

While we often manifest without being aware of it, our focus here is on Inspired Manifestation. Since we are always bringing something to life, why not deliver what is most satisfying and personally enriching, which also fulfills our Soul's Purposes? Then the question becomes: How do we shift from our default mode of unconscious manifesting to a more conscious, deliberate, preferred manifestation? Destiny.

Destiny Makes Manifesting More Deliberate

Destiny implies a destination or place of arrival, and also literally means "from the stars," suggesting that we are heading toward a stellar place that has been Divinely designed. Our destiny is encoded in our Soul's blueprint, impressed in the fibers of our being at the inception of our Soul. It determines how we unleash the infinite love within for our own benefit, and all of life. Destiny comes quite naturally to us; it is an inevitable consequence of becoming who we are. The central opportunity of Destiny is to personally experience, express and enjoy unconditional love.

The seeds of our Destiny are embedded within the fabric of our Soul. Composed of the elements required to realize our destination, the Soul is infused with intention, purpose, potential, possibility, talent, desire, interest and inclination—all necessary to arrive in a location perfectly fitting every need and fulfilling all promises of each particular incarnation as well as our entire Soul's journey. Every subtle shade of possibility, given the reality of who we are in this lifetime, is factored into our destiny. While it may seem accidental, or coincidental, it is deliberate. Our opportunity at this stage of human evolution is to be conscious as we inhabit it.

Our ultimate Destiny is both universal and personal. At the universal level, our collective destination is a state of unconditional self-love: freely loving all as is. Our ultimate Destiny includes a state of unity where all people experience, express and enjoy unconditional love, and participate and contribute in nurturing and satisfying ways. Our individual destiny is the activation of our Divine potential— our particular pattern through which Divine light shines—so that we can love and enjoy who we are and at the same time, the world is positively affected by the specific contribution that only we can make. The seeds of our personal destination are within us, making it possible for us to grow in the direction of our destiny. Because this potential exists, it guides us one decision at a time.

Destiny is a natural consequence of the relationship between our Soul's Purposes, our human self and the Divine. Just as a tomato plant sprouts from a tomato seed, a cow births a calf, and a cloud releases rain when moist air passes a certain threshold, we become who we are destined to be. Our destiny cannot be imposed upon us by anyone else; it is revealed through us and emerges as us in real-time and space. Our destiny does not operate outside or separate from us; it is already present within us from birth. We are always growing into our potential, as more is revealed.

Our personal comfort with paradox supports the recognition of our destiny and helps us make conscious strides towards our optimal experience. Standing in both spiritual and human dimensions of self, appreciating each on its own as well as the shared partnership, we straddle a powerful paradox. Imagine laying the infinity symbol on the ground and placing a foot in each circle.

As you straddle the two (representing a paradox), locate your zone of personal gravity. Notice how your inner resources become enlivened by the opportunity to be fully spiritual while also completely human. Opening to the sacred marriage of Soul and the human body, your inevitable destiny ignites.

Even if you are somehow content in this moment, it seems that everyone else on our planet is clamoring for more. Because it is the nature of life to always be expanding, as we achieve one goal, another comes into our awareness. This is evidence that we are alive and in harmony with the nature of life. As a matter of fact, those of us involved in awakening spiritual awareness came to the planet at this time precisely so that we can actively participate in this epic shift.

These insights have given me such tremendous relief—as I hope and trust they will help you, too. Knowing that life in its infinite mercy and compassion is supporting me, I can engage more fully. Noticing what I am manifesting, I adjust my understanding, giving form to my moment-by-moment interpretations. Because manifesting is an ongoing process, I expect evaluation and adjustment. You, too, should be willing to review and update your avenues for expression so that they remain appropriate to your particular life stage. The only constant is change.

In our next exercise, we consider what might be our Soul's Purposes from yet another point of view. We are beginning to understand that our Soul's Purposes are a natural part of us. It's not that they are "near and dear," which implies that they are somehow separate from us. In truth, they are our natural potentials given who we are as human beings at this point in time, here on earth. Let's take another look at what they might be.

Exercise: Another Look at Your Soul's Purposes: Shining Light on Your Soul's Purposes

Open your Records. With your eyes closed, open your awareness. Get a sense of the presence of that sacred aspect of your being, that part that is never pushy or demanding, but instead, quietly makes itself known without imposing or invading your customary relationship with yourself. In the space of spiritual truth and compassion, consider that there exists a reservoir of infinite, eternal support for you. It is dedicated to you and your personal evolution throughout your Soul's journey as a human. That well of wisdom is on hand for you, here and now.

Whether with great certainty or imagination, think back to yourself coming into this life as a baby with remarkable potential, full of possibilities for this incarnation, born into the pure light of life. It may seem to be a spotlight, pure and powerful, with your infant self right in the middle. If you can't actually see this image, don't worry. It's perfectly acceptable to imagine this scenario. Looking at your infant self, what do you recognize as some of the obvious possibilities you were carrying in your heart and Soul? It could be anything: a love of music, a talent for building things, an ability to dance. Ask for illumination to identify some of the dreams, hopes and wishes you brought into this life. These are some of the particular reasons your Soul, in partnership with the Divine, selected you to make these ideals a reality.

Now, see if you can get a glimpse of yourself as a child, up until age 7. You might see images or simply feel your child self. Either way is fine. Keeping your child self in the spotlight that is pure, powerful spiritual light will make it easier for you to glimpse the potential you had as a child. All of your talents, interests, dreams, hopes, and wishes are important expressions of your Soul's Purposes.

Continuing on through the years, invite the light to shine through your memory to help you to recall those ideas you've been holding in your heart for your whole life. What did you hope to accomplish, dream about achieving, wish would happen? Keep considering through your teen years into your young adulthood. There were some things you wanted to experience in this life. Maybe you took action, maybe you were unable to take action. Either way, those hopes were in your heart. Observe the ways in which your relationship with your Soul's Purposes has developed in this life. Keep the light shining on yourself and your life up to the present. In this pure spiritual light, where the goodness of everything is understood, let yourself recall those dreams, desires, hopes and wishes you've been holding within.

Consider the power of your cherished ideals, those particular possibilities that are so precious they have persisted throughout every event of your life. You've lived a full life with so many experiences—what dreams are still alive within you? Invite the light to shine on the ways in which some of the desires of your heart have been able to stay alive throughout your life. At times you felt they were impossible to achieve and tucked them away in the far reaches of your mind. At other times, other matters were much more important. There may even be times when you tried to forget them! Notice the persistent quality of a special handful of cherished dreams that have been with you for your entire life.

Yes, it's also true that there are some heartfelt desires you have manifested. Let the light shine on these, so you can clearly identify what has already come to pass. Some of your treasured ideals have been brought to life and you have been amply blessed by these experiences. Notice how wonderful it is for you when you are able to manifest some of your most treasured dreams. Beautiful!

At this time, let yourself become aware of the resilient, durable, tenacious nature of your Soul's Purposes. Acknowledge yourself for those you've already manifested and for those yet to materialize. It's fascinating to notice that there are some desires we safeguard, even when unable to realize, and they accompany us throughout our journey—raising many questions. What could possibly be in our way and why? We are not stupid creatures. There must be positive, valid reasons for not allowing ourselves to proceed with our dreams or have our hearts desires. What's in the way?

This is a good time to close your Records using the Pathway Prayer Process©.

After the Exercise

You've been so dedicated to finding out the truth about yourself, your character traits, beliefs and interpretations that were once such a fitting way to take care of yourself. Your willingness to be honest and kind is profound, and the precise combination necessary to stimulate your success. Now we are seeing that we've outgrown many of our old ideas, and what was once a support has become a restriction. It is perfectly sound to edit the fundamental notions preventing your growth into higher goodness. Along the way to bringing our Soul's Purposes to life, we have the chance to refresh our rendering of interpretations of ourselves, others and circumstances we've encountered. Additionally, we can do the same for our understanding of the obstacles in our way. Let's consider obstacles and obstructions through the Akashic lens.

12

Clearing Obstacles to Manifest Your Destiny

Permanent, sustainable transformation requires that both inner and outer aspects be addressed. Obstructions are outer aspects, grievances against the self are inner aspects. Then, there's the matter of stuck trauma and our personal understanding and relationship to manifesting. Let's look first at obstructions.

Obstructions

An obstruction is something blocking, an obstacle. It impedes, hinders, thwarts or interferes. An obstacle is something standing in the way or opposing our ideal. As we come to believe that life is on our side, that there is a law of life at work. Demanding that everything occurring is for our good or benefit, we need to consider obstructions from a new point of view. What if every obstacle was somehow our ally, assisting us in mysterious ways, keeping us safe, helping us? But what could be some realistic reasons for preventing ourselves from having what we want? What if our dream is not really ours, but our spouse's or our parents? Maybe we feel it's more spiritual to be deprived than fulfilled. Or it's better to find happiness even though we are miserable.

Let's examine some possible reasons for obstruction. Maybe we are not being honest with ourselves. Maybe we allow obstacles because we are afraid to have what we want. It's easy to become convinced that being fulfilled will be harmful, particularly when our desired outcome seems impossible. We may choose to deny the existence of an impossible dream rather than risk failing.

I've worked with students who have sincerely tried to eliminate obstacles based on the idea that they were a pesky nuisance—to no avail. Perhaps we parrot the words of someone we admire and speak about their dreams, hoping they will love us. If we negatively assess our dream or ourselves for having the dream, we cannot possibly realize it. We won't allow ourselves to achieve something we deem dangerous. If we consider ourselves to be unworthy or inadequate for the task, it cancels out hope. If we think the dream is foolish, it becomes inert. As long as we harshly judge either the dream or the dreamer, we won't achieve the dream. Our negative judgments bring progress to a screeching halt. It's also possible to allow or even co-create obstacles. Guilt, fear, and unworthiness can get in the way. Unresolved past life issues, ingrained ancestral patterns, or calcified patterns of behavior will thwart our efforts.

With options for obstructions numbering as many as there are individuals, the question becomes, "Why would we do this to ourselves?" Let's remember this: we create obstacles because we believe they are good for us. There is no outside force dedicated to depriving us of our dreams. Maybe we believe that it is better to be deprived or denied our dreams, that somehow we are more evolved if unattached to our heart's deepest desires, or that it is more virtuous to be in a state of unrequited love, to be fulfilled at a later date. We are evolving past beliefs long held by humans ascribing punitive, cruel motives to unseen gods, essentially expressing our own human fears and confusion, relinquishing ideas of unworthiness and depravity.

Is it possible we have these obstructions because they are somehow helping us? Perhaps we need to reconsider our obstructions, and look for all the good reasons we have them. Likely, we are required to make peace with ourselves for the choice of our obstructions, and accept the gifts of the obstacles themselves.

As we honor and appreciate these seeming limitations, we can grow through them. In the process, obstructions dissolve and new possibilities emerge. Contrary to many traditional religious beliefs, there is no god or outside force that wants to deprive or punish us. It's more likely we do not have what we want because we are afraid (for some valid but unknown reason) to have it. One of the great laws of life is that we only, but always, allow ourselves to have what we want when we are convinced that it is in our best interest to have it.

Acceptance is the Key!

Acceptance facilitates release, freeing us to move along our path. No matter what you have done or failed to do, the goal is to find a way to accept and align with yourself, even if you are not pleased with your own behavior or predicament. Remember that we always make choices in our best interest, believing that the decisions will increase our experience of love—no exceptions.

Awakening to our inherent, essential goodness, appreciating our innate value and connecting to our heart's desire, we can begin to enjoy unconditional love for self, others and the whole of creation. As we make peace with who we are, our destiny naturally emerges. As our conscious understanding catches up to our ideals, our dreams begin to come true. Rooted in this new perspective, we begin to see that obstacles are on our path to help us. Reconsidering our obstructions as good, we begin to look for the good and see that life is conspiring with us to fulfill our Soul's Purposes and manifest our destiny. Accelerating the process of release begins by recognizing the wisdom of our willingness to allow ourselves to retain an obstacle.

Understanding that our selecting the obstruction was the most self-loving option at the time we made the choice (or we would have picked something else). And letting ourselves become consciously aware of the ways in which the obstacle has served us, accepting and appreciative of ourselves and the obstacle, the obstacle begins to dissolve, and we move into greater freedom.

Grievances

With innate love and our dreams and desires latent within us, what could possibly get in the way of manifesting our Soul's Purposes and fulfilling our Destiny? The secret treasures of our heart persist throughout hardships of every variety, the pulse of our dreams throbs in the background of stress and monotony of grueling phases of human living and, yet, these durable treasures reside in a no-man's land where they do not come to fruition, nor do they wither and die. What could thwart these enduring possibilities? And delaying these inevitabilities?

Plenty, as it turns out! Let's consider the number one obstacle: grievances against the self. This includes complaints, self-condemnation, rejection and all other forms of negative judgments. In whatever form, these obstacles prevent us from experiencing our full potential. In fact, they keep us attached to the object of our disdain.

Grievances are the flip side of the obstacle coin, the inner aspect of an obstacle. A grievance is a cause for distress, providing a valid reason for a complaint. A complaint is an expression of pain or dissatisfaction that is holding us back from realizing our dreams. Self-condemnation or rejection in any form will always prevent us from experiencing our potential. Negative judgment keeps us attached to the object of our disdain. Acceptance (not approval) facilitates release, freeing us to move along our life path. The opportunity at hand is to get on our own side, no matter what we have done or failed to do. There is a way to align with yourself, even if you are not especially pleased with your own behavior or predicament. Stretch to understand your own reasoning. Understand we are always making choices that we believe will activate a more potent experience of love. No exceptions!

Let's consider grievances we inflict upon ourselves. Self-criticism holds us back more than anything else, preventing us from experiencing our full potential. Unattainable standards of perfection keep us stuck in a cyclical pattern of painful behavior. In fact, negative judgment acts like glue, keeping us attached to the object of our disdain, while acceptance (a recognition of what is happening) facilitates release, liberating us to move along our life path.

At some point, we will be challenged to make peace with our perfectly imperfect human selves. From the perspective of reincarnation, the purpose of our Soul's journey through our human experience is to know and love ourselves no matter what. Within each individual human incarnation, our primary opportunity is to expand our experience of unconditional self-love—to learn to love ourselves in all situations, and under all conditions. Becoming more aware of the Divine within, we begin to master the spiritual practice of unconditional self-love, knowing and loving ourselves as we are known and loved by the Divine.

I think that the single most transformational idea is unconditional self-love as a spiritual practice. This radical idea wasn't even an option until the last century, at the time of the splitting of the atom, with the rise of authoritarianism in between the two world wars. The invitation here is to befriend yourself no matter what you have/not done, especially if you are not pleased with your behavior or predicament. Say to yourself something that carries the sentiment of, "It's okay. Even though I was _____, I understand. Of course, it seemed like a good idea at the time or I would not have done it." The feeling is far more important than any specific words. Use whatever words help you feel loved and understood.

No matter what the behavior, we chose it because we believed it to be our best option at the time. Every pattern is positive at its point of origin. We select behaviors that seem to be good solutions to the problems we face at the time. No person ever deliberately intends or chooses to cause themselves harm. Even people who self-harm by cutting do it because they want to feel better. Condemning yourself is so painful, and it's not a productive strategy for achieving your dreams

To release yourself from this bind, ask, "How do I love myself even though ...? How do I extend kindness and respect to myself even though ...?" We are not denying our imperfections, we are acknowledging our human fragility without indignation or offense, allowing ourselves to be as we are in the present. Don't wait any longer to extend kindness and respect to yourself. You may be surprised that once compassion, understanding and love are offered, the malady often resolves. Love satisfies a myriad of human needs.

Our default approach to transformation by criticism was a common idea for centuries. It was the best, most positive and loving idea we humans had. Rooted in a dim opinion of ourselves as humans, it made good sense that our strategies for self-improvement, and relationship with others were based on the notion that humans are inherently flawed, even bad, deserving of a good kick in the pants to get moving and improve. This concept was actually helpful for some people, some of the time. But the cloud of negative perception hovering over humans had limited results. After a time, this critical point of view caused a halt in our transformation, because being condemned is just too painful.

It's only in the last 100 years that the idea that humans are inherently good, composed of love at the core of our being, has come into our collective consciousness. This radical assumption about human nature upends just about every idea we have about who we are, what makes us tick and what ignites our growth into our potential. Glimpsing our own goodness, as scandalous as that may seem brings a transformational heat to the latent riches we've been cultivating within our character for lifetimes. Surprisingly, it turns out for many that acceptance, kindness and respect, understanding and patience activate our finest human qualities, and inspire us to share the best of who we are with the world. In the process, the pesky limitations begin to fade away, shrinking into the withered state they merit.

We must be realistic about the rate of progress as we move along the spiritual pathway into experiencing unconditional self-love. We know that somewhere deep within we already love ourselves. The opportunity is to grow into this potential, the seeds already planted in the nature of our being. As this is a natural growth pattern, we have to grow into it organically, over time. While we have the template for 100% unconditional love for self, others and all of creation infused into the nature of our being, our task is to bring this spiritual, Soul-level awareness to our human reality. This is the essence of manifesting—to bring the consciousness of our Soul to life through our human self, into the ordinary world. It's quite easy to revel in the attributes of love when we are not in bodies, with mortgages and teenagers. However, it's a heroic challenge for the awakening individual to deliberately, conscientiously move through our human experience fully aware, and participating in the spiritual process underpinning it all. Remember that, from a Soul-level perspective, as we travel from lifetime to lifetime, we expand our experience of unconditional self-love, awakening to more of our whole self.

I offer these helpful strategies for success:

- Begin where you are. There is no better time or place to start!
- Take one baby step at a time. Small actions help us to manage potential risk, observe the results, and take good care of our emotions as they surface.
- Do what you can with what you have. You already have all the talent and desire, put it to work so it can expand! Life does not wish you to debt yourself or harm yourself in any way. This is your chance to be creative!
- Ask for help when needed. There's just no reason not to ask for help from people who can actually be of assistance. Don't

deprive yourself of the opportunity to ask, receive, empower yourself and the giver. It's the circle of life and, since you already belong, enjoy it! This just may be the excuse you need to activate the connections between you and others!

- Be patient—it will take longer than you think. Everything takes time here on earth! But once you embark on the great adventure, time as you know it will shift and become your friend. There is always enough time to move in the direction of your dreams!

- You will make mistakes. For me, this is a great lesson in humility. Mistakes are part of the journey, not an exception and certainly not punitive. Whenever we are alive, we live with the capacity for error. The point is not perfection, but pleasurable usefulness! Make peace with human imperfection, it's not personal! Take responsibility for your part of any mess, apologize quickly, give yourself a break and be sure to give the same forgiveness to everyone else. Let it go and move on! Don't be too shocked when the next error comes to your attention. It's alright!

- Keep going—Never give up! One of the great features of our Soul's Purposes is that they just don't leave us alone! They live within us, demanding our attention until we take them seriously. Inner peace necessitates some awareness and action regarding our purposes. It does not demand completion, simply acceptance followed by action, all to the best of our ability. Don't ever give up permanently—it won't make you happy!

Exercise: Transform Your Relationships with Obstacles & Grievances

Now, let's get our Akashic Records open using the Pathway Prayer Process©. Here's a practice to help you achieve the freedom you want. It's your right!

Relax into the sanctuary of infinite kindness, respect and understanding that is your own sacred space. Expand your awareness to detect the presence of the light, and your personal place within that light. In this loving atmosphere, describe your favorite, most cherished dream for yourself in this life. For this exercise, it's best to contemplate something that is very meaningful to you, something that you have wanted for your whole life. Please keep your focus on this lifetime. When did you become aware of this possibility? What is it? Describe what you want as if you were in a conversation with a new friend, tell them what it is that you are hoping to experience in this life. Elaborate on the plans you've made to have this happen, the actions you've taken, the failures you've had, as well as the successful parts.

As we survey your journey with this particular possibility, this purpose of your Soul: What do you recognize as obstructions or obstacles to your success? What interferes or prevents your fulfillment of this desire? Perhaps you are lacking some skills or education that would be helpful. It's possible your fears are crippling but try to identify what you are afraid of. What people, places or circumstances outside of you are hindering you? What traits, characteristics, qualities, conditions (education or money) within you are thwarting your dreams?

Now, let's pretend these obstructions are actually helping you. How are they guiding or directing your quest? Imagine you arranged for these hurdles for some very good reason. You're not stupid. In fact, you love yourself and are ALWAYS striving to provide more love to yourself. Is it possible that these obstructions are somehow assisting you on this journey? Intensify the spiritual light to empower your perception. Can you sense/see any way in which these obstructions have been your trusted allies, helping you become your more loving self in this life?

We're going to shift gears just a little bit. Throughout your life, you have made some decisions that have not brought about your desired results, and you've taken actions leading to unfortunate circumstances, and causing you to be upset with yourself. Bring to mind some choice you made that led you away from your desire, rather than toward it. You may have done something that you are unhappy about, or avoided taking action when it would have brought you to your preferred intention much sooner. In the merciful and pure spiritual light, notice if you had any other viable options at the time. Can you see/sense that your selection was actually the best idea you had at the time? Something about it was compelling. What drew you to make this choice?

Consider the ways in which your response was helpful at the time. Do your best to be compassionate and understanding with yourself. If you have difficulty being sincerely kind and respectful, ask the light, which has been your constant companion, to assist you. Are you willing to treat yourself with respect and dignity even though you are not perfect? Can you grasp the perfection of your actions that seem to be mistakes? Are you open to manifesting your dreams even though you are imperfect, and sometimes make mistakes? And of course, are you willing to be loving to others, to participate in life even though you have not yet manifested your treasured Soul's Purposes yet? And so, for now, in gratitude and with humility, we let this be.

Close your Records simply by reading the Closing Prayer out loud. A few minutes of grounding yourself can help after an important inquiry.

After the Exercise

Another way to examine these complicating factors is to consider our relationship with universal fears and traumas. We are naturally part of the wave of collective terrors about living and dying. These have a surprisingly powerful impact on us, so it's in our best interest to become aware of them. With awareness, we increase the potency of our choices. Fear of living can result in refusal to take necessary action, pretending we are not interested in our most cherished dream, or simply having a terrible time getting started on things even when they are important to us. The fear of dying can influence us in the opposite ways. We can struggle with completing projects, or get very sloppy toward and ruin our hard-won efforts.

We have a chance in our next exercise to explore our own patterns with these, and to initiate letting them go, which will set the pace for new manifestation. This particular inquiry can be uncomfortable, but it's well worth it. Making peace with who we have been in other times and places, and cultivating appreciation and understanding for the choices we made and decisions about ourselves, others, is transformational. As always, we'll be together as we continue on our amazing Akashic adventure.

Exercise: Releasing Stuck Traumas

For this exercise, be sure to allow ample time for the treasures of your ancient insights and wisdom to come into focus. Say the Prayer following the instructions to open your Akashic Records.

Settle into your spiritual safe space, opening up to the amplified sense of compassion and dignity. Resting in this realm, it's very likely you can detect a sphere of light surrounding you, and the pillar of light within you, anchored at your root, extending out through the crown of your head. This inner pillar holds the major energy centers, your chakras, in their place. You may never see them, but they are always there, working to maintain the flow of the life force through you as you live your life.

Now, open your awareness so you can recognize some of the ways in which you carry ancient, universal fears of living and dying. Perhaps you are anxious about starting new projects, preferring instead to continue with activities that are familiar, even when they're no longer satisfying. You may do this with your work, or even in relationships. Maybe you start things and when they become difficult, you stop and move on to something new. Or you may be afraid that your ideas will be harmful to yourself or other people. It may be easier to pretend you don't want to move forward because you don't want to inconvenience anyone. Just get a sense of your general pattern with regard to initiating new projects, or pursuing your dreams in this life. Good.

Now turn your attention to your customary behavior with regard to completing projects. You may dread finishing, and do all kinds of things to prolong a project, or keep a relationship going even though no one is happy. Or, you may find yourself rushing to finish and becoming sloppy with the details. Some of us avoid fulfilling our dreams and simply want to finish up whether the project is, ready or not. Again, we want a general sense of your standard pattern with regard to completing projects, or fulfilling your dreams.

Now direct your attention into the inner pillar of light at the core of your being. Focus on the root, or entry point at the base of your physical body. Our dedicated awareness initiates the opening of the root chakra so we can explore those birth experiences having the most impact on us in this life. Here we find that you have had a great variety of experiences being born. Some are so easy, elegant and graceful. You have had lifetimes of being very excited about being born, and others full of dread. Sometimes, your mother was young, healthy and strong, with an easy birth. And, other times, your mother was sick or frail; maybe she did not survive the delivery. All of us have had a full spectrum of birth experiences.

Scanning this series of births, notice one that is outstanding. Is there a prior birth experience that is having a negative influence on you in this life? Observe the circumstances. What happened? How did you respond? What decisions did you make about yourself? About life? Maybe your mother died, and you felt so terrible you decided you would never do anything to upset anyone, and so you have been unable to manifest your dreams. Whatever occurred, can you extend love and compassion to yourself? Now, let that experience go.

Next, let's look for a positive birth experience—one in which you were delighted, as were your parents. You felt you were bringing love and coming home to a completely loving environment. It was wonderful. Take a moment to allow yourself to feel how magnificent it was to be so conscious of the infinite love all around you. At this time, let this infusion of love permeate every cell of your being. Now, let the experience go but let the love remain.

Take a deep breath. At this time, we allow our awareness to travel to the crown chakra, the top of our heads—this is the point of our departure or death. Your dedicated awareness naturally stimulates this energy center, the one holding the memories of all the deaths you've ever had, so you can find which ones are most influential in this incarnation. As with your birth experiences, you have had every type of death imaginable. Some were surrounded by peace and love, painless and graceful. Other times, you died suddenly as a youth, or even a middle-aged person. Some lifetimes, you were elderly, sick and alone. There were lifetimes when you were tired and grateful to be moving along to your next experience. And of course, some lifetimes when you were heartbroken that you had to leave. One of these deaths stands out more than the others, one that is having a negative, limiting impact on you in this life. Notice the circumstances. What happened? How did you respond? What decisions did you make about yourself and life? Maybe you determined that life was not fair, and it was better for you to not even bother participating? Or that it was too hard, too painful and you would rather not take any chances. You may have died in war with overwhelming feelings of hopelessness. There are many possibilities. Can you love yourself even though you were in a terrible situation? Can you love yourself even though you died in a tragic way? Now, let that go.

Let's turn our attention toward another death experience, a positive one. Look within so you can identify a positive death—one in which you were at peace, unafraid and willing to go to your next incarnation. You may have been alone or with loved ones, but you were totally clear about the love in your own heart and the love circulating throughout every life circumstance. You were confident in the reality of love. Take a moment to allow yourself to relish this experience. You knew then that love would never die, you felt yourself a being of love, in a sea of love. It was marvelous. Let your understanding of the situation fall away, but allow the living love to remain. Move now into the cave of your heart. Let your awareness of the inner pillar fade away, your recollection of difficult passages, birth and death dissolve, until all that remains is love. You, as a being of love, exist in a universe of love—unconditionally loving yourself through hardships and joys. And, in so doing, the limitations of ancient difficulties dissolve and you, my friend, are free. And so, for now, we leave this be. All that remains is love.

Before we leave the Akasha, let's bathe in the essence of your inner reality, the love. It's yours, and has been for as long as you've been in existence, and will remain for eternity. Both infinitely potent, and totally invisible to the human eye. Enjoy it! It's yours. When you're ready, close your Records and ground yourself in your everyday existence.

After the Exercise

At this juncture of our journey, we are right in the middle of "clearing"— finding ways to make sense of our choices, relinquish harsh interpretations and surrender harmful perspectives. Clearing is valuable for us because all the light/love of life is alive and well within us. Every dream stimulating the life force is there. These are present because you are the ideal individual to experience, express and enjoy these very specific activities. The desires of your heart reside within you because you are the right person to bring them to life, no matter what opinion you hold about yourself. As we make peace with who we are as people, recognizing ourselves from an altitude of mercy and appreciation, our authentic destiny emerges. When our conscious understanding catches up to our ideals, these dreams begin to come true.

Summing Up

We live in times hyper focused on Manifesting. As a material goal, it can be competitive and demoralizing. There are always those with more and, at the same time, those with less. Manifesting in the 21st century is a spiritual venture. When we deliberately engage in bringing our Soul's Purposes to life, the realm of manifesting dramatically changes—sometimes resulting in more material success than we ever expected. Spiritual manifesting is our opportunity to experience and express the unlimited love within us—in our own individual manner. Even if we are basically content, the entire planet is clamoring for authentic, fulfilling manifestation. It is the nature of life to always be expanding, so once we achieve a goal, you can be sure another one is on its way! Happily, this is not an indication of a problem but rather, evidence that we are fully alive, growing and in harmony with the nature of life. For all of us active in the awakening of their spiritual awareness, we came to earth at this time so we could actively participate in this epic collective leap, by contributing our personal manifestation of our own Soul's Purposes to the wave.

Inspired Manifestation, therefore, is the process through which we bring our Soul's Purposes to life. This avenue is an outgrowth of our will. The will is the point where our Soul engages with planetary life, it is the place where our deepest dreams connect with the life in which we find ourselves. As we humans are recognizing the will and its nature, our urgency to manifest becomes more insistent. In ages past, most of us felt that a rare handful of exceptional individuals would accomplish their dreams, and didn't count ourselves among that group. Others tried to force their personal hopes onto others with unfortunate consequences.

But now, we are in a new age, one in which the imperative is to bring our treasured dreams to life and give them form, by finding ways to harmoniously interact in the world. In order to manifest, we must believe that it is beneficial for us personally, as well as others. This is not a case of 100% fierce conviction, but a matter of 51% of our self must be convinced that it is in our best interest to manifest our intention. This is because we only (but always) allow ourselves to be, do and have those things we deem good. While we may think manifesting is a swell idea, our old ideas and fears can be lurking around preventing our progress.

In our next chapter, we'll examine this situation and initiate its resolution.

13

Robust Manifesting: Money, Prosperity & Abundance

All of this spiritual conversation sounds wonderful—but what about money, prosperity and abundance? You may have thought we would never get to this part of the work, but here we are! Let's begin by exploring some basic terms, all of which are subjective, and only truly defined by each of us.

Money is a Medium of Exchange

Energetically, we trade our energy (our gifts, talents and abilities) for money, which positions us to use money to trade for the gifts, talents and abilities of others. Money allows us to give and receive. None of us can do everything, nor should we, and so we are here to discover ways to interact and find our place in the circle of life. One great thing about money is that it simplifies our exchanges. I like to think that the circulation of money is a manifestation of our interdependent relationships with other people around the world, reminding us that we are part of one whole.

Prosperity

The constantly changing condition of thriving, flourishing, experiencing success, sometimes experienced as economic well-being, but also inclusive of many other experiences of abundance, is prosperity. Prosperity is always experienced in the moment and can include: a network of friends, the freedom to travel, barter systems, opportunities to serve others, the freedom to express and so many others.

Fulfillment is a magnet for prosperity. As we give the best of who we are to life, we feel fulfilled, and life responds accordingly. We prosper. When I say, "Yes" to the central inquiry of this book—Am I willing to experience and express love? Am I willing to experience unconditional love for myself, others and all of creation?—I expand my experience of personal fulfillment, and prosperity results.

Abundance: Having More Than Enough

This cannot be objectively determined; it is a personal, subjective sense. I have known artists who live entirely off the grid, with no assets whatsoever, who feel abundant and I have met millionaires living in the lap of luxury by any measurable standard, with enough in the bank to support lifetimes, who feel like they never have enough. A dear friend who spent years in an orphanage, and then years in jail, now travels the world painting youth hostels. He cherishes his freedom working in the gig economy, and frequently tells me he could not be happier.

Over the years, it has become quite popular to use money, prosperity and abundance as indicators of spiritual fitness. We have to be compassionate with ourselves, as we are in a significant growth phase as humans, and easily confused. We have, for centuries, assumed that the gods showered favor on the rich, that the wealthy were more enlightened than the rest, perhaps earning an exemption from human troubles. The flip side of that coin was that the poor must be sinners, criminals from other incarnations, terribly flawed and deserving of their destitute condition. For some of us, these cultural standards may seem like they belong to others but, at some level, we believe them, or have in the past. And now is the time to consciously relinquish these judgmental, erroneous notions, opening our minds and hearts to a deeper truth.

Fulfillment & Satisfaction

Have you ever felt like "I have everything I need, so why do I feel so empty?" Our fulfillment and satisfaction seem to have little to do with amounts of money. Actually, as we are involved in meaningful pursuits and activities, money assumes its proper place: as a tool to support our experience of life. We know that living costs money, and part of our human adventure is learning how to contribute to our world, interact with others and provide for our earthly needs. Money is a part of the landscape, but it is not the determinant of our value. Our confusion is to be expected. Many religions suggest that prosperity is evidence of divine preference or spiritual illumination. Curiously, other religions—sometimes the very same ones—infer that there is spiritual value in poverty. Both interpretations can be used to evidence our unworthiness or our uniqueness, and both fortify our confusion about separation. Applying a dualistic construct, we expect this.

It also follows that many of us are obsessed with manifesting money. Here's the truth: money is not an indicator of spiritual fitness. When you don't have it, money sure seems like a big deal. I get it. I have certainly struggled with confusion about prosperity over the years. I can remember thinking that money would find me if I was spiritual enough, and then I could buy a condo in Hawaii and sit on the beach, drinking iced tea all day. Recently, I was invited to teach at a glitzy resort in paradise (as defined by cultural glamour standards). It was lovely, but it was not my personal paradise! There was no extra level of spiritual awareness there, simply human beings enjoying a high level of personal comfort.

A fundamental problem with the passive "money will find me" approach is that it actually undermines our efforts to manifest. Inspired Manifestation will not happen without a robust willingness to do what is needed. Remember the Triangle Test requirements for manifestation (heart + mind + will). Will is precisely what puts the manifestation process in motion, and also the energy that keeps it rolling forward. When not regularly used, our will has a tendency to atrophy. For perpetual transformation to occur, will must be consistently present; effort is required. Effort is not punishment. Life is meant to be lived. Very few people are here on earth to sit and meditate, drink tea and stare out the window. Most of us are on the planet to learn how to interact and engage in ways that activate the infinite love within, and that requires action.

Action is good and often fun, whether household chores, running a business or contributing to civic needs. Through action, we learn who we are, what inspires us and how we can effectively participate in the world. Thinking about it is a good start, having positive feelings toward it is another positive step, but action is the magic word. Through action, our essence co-mingles with the essence of life. We become co-creators, neither victims being trampled by life or bullies imposing our will on the world. Expect to discover harmony in the Realm of Engagement.

Liberating Ideas

Over the years on my journey of expanding awareness, I have learned some liberating ideas that dismantle these outdated perspectives. First, I was challenged to reconsider the purpose of increasing spiritual awareness—to accelerate our experience of unconditional love—not to make money. The Universe is invested in us and our dreams, hopes, potentials and desires. The Universe is committed to each of us awakening to our lovability, and will always provide the resources we need to bring forth who we are, so we can effectively participate in life and deliver the contribution carried in our hearts. In every lifetime, we have numerous opportunities to know the truth about ourselves, aligning our awareness and actions with the Divine. Sometimes, this involves having money. Other times, it involves minimal resources. The key questions are these: Can I love myself when I am rich? Can I love myself when I am poor? Can I let myself participate in life, engage with other people no matter what my bank account says?

As spiritual creatures aware of our spiritual essence, amazing possibilities await. Making money is not our Soul's Purpose. It is absolutely true that having more than enough money positions us to initiate immense good in the world, whether through charity, a humanitarian project, the arts, education or any institute through which we experience. Even in cases like this, the money is not the goal, but the means to the end. And what is shockingly powerful is that if we deliberately allow ourselves to begin where we are, with what we have, searching for ways to experience and express our purposes within our limited means, the avenue through which funds travel can more easily find us.

Money is simply a tool for interacting with each other, and then gathering and organizing the resources needed to bring our Soul's Purposes to life. Life always provides sufficient funds for our next step, not magically, but through everyday channels. Clarifying our dreams, treating our treasured desires with respect, taking action to the best of our ability, trusting, knowing that life is on our side. This conscious relationship connects us with the funds we need to continue on our path. Not to accomplish the entire project, but always to take the next right step. Even though we are here to interact with each other, and to provide support for each other's work in the world, It is worth noting that we cannot profit on someone else's Soul's Purposes. Prosperity and abundance come solely from fulfillment with our own Soul's Purposes.

Think of all the imperfect people who have made amazing contributions to the world. There are the "greats" (Einstein, etc.) and then there are the countless regular human beings daring to love, share, enjoy, contribute and participate without waiting for some elusive perfection to be bestowed on them. Some of us will accomplish tremendous feats while here on earth, most of us will not. Amazingly, none of us is barred from being happy, or enjoying the lives we are living. We can have a good day no matter how much cash is in our piggy bank. Without exception, all of us have the chance to love and be loved, to share and participate—just the way we are. Unlimited goodness shines through limited humans, that's just the way it is. We might as well enjoy it.

Truly, if we need money to experience and express our Soul's Purposes, we have it—but only enough for the moment. We do not amass money and then figure out how to use it. Unless of course, we are having that type of lifetime, in which case we are still charged with identifying what activates the infinite love within us, and what activities empower us to share that love with others. But we always have sufficient funds to initiate the process.

Money is a resource we can use to help us express our Soul's Purposes. Life is dedicated to us realizing our value, and sharing ourselves in the world. When we are engaged in the process of bringing our Soul's intentions to life, the required resources become available to us, and it will always be satisfying. There is always enough of what we really desire. And the flip side is that there is never enough of what we don't want.

Unconditional self-love is an overarching/underlying Soul's Purposes for all humans on their journey. We are challenged to learn to love ourselves, treating ourselves with kindness, respect, patience and appreciation in any and all circumstances. This can translate into some lifetimes learning to love and respect ourselves when we are poor or rich, depending on where our prejudices reside.

We are engaged in a deliberate process to become fully aware of who we are and have been in our relationship with money. Gathering these insights requires looking at this matter from a variety of angles, raising a range of questions designed to bring our inner truths to surface so we can get a good idea of what's stored within. It's beneficial to do these exercises over time, and repeatedly, to give yourself the time and space a human being requires to adjust our perspective, learn how to decipher and value the wisdom imparted. Trying to peel all the skin off the onion in one sitting is a nice idea, but impractical for most of us as we give our emotions an opportunity to integrate our awareness. We move now to another inquiry into our inner truths about our connections to money.

Exercise: Your Relationship with Money; Impressions Through Spiritual Light

Open your Akashic Records using the Pathway Prayer Process© and, when you are ready, move into the deep spiritual water of this Realm.

As your eyes close, the inner light turns on. Settle into this space of safety and understanding. We begin this time by taking a quick glimpse at your infant self when you first arrived on the planet this time. It's perfectly acceptable to imagine this. How much cash did you have when you got here? Any investments or property? When your time here is complete, how much money will you be able to transfer into your future? Beautiful. Let this go. Let's move quickly through these prompts. No need to dwell or ruminate. Glimpse. Grasp. Release and move on.

It can be challenging to be asked to simply "glimpse, release and move on." But, this is exactly what this practice asks of us. Some of the prompts will trigger recollections, others may not. This is not the practice for in-depth probing of our motivations. Rather, it is designed to stimulate ancient memories of moments stored in the treasury of your Soul, affecting you to this very day. Simply do your best with this. Trust that what you need to know will be revealed in the best possible manner.

Every one of us has been gifted with an imagination. In this particular guided practice, we use imagination to support the expansion of our awareness. Imagination is a doorway to the spiritual dimension, providing every individual his or her own launching pad from ordinary states of consciousness to extraordinary states. As we examine our relationship with money, we also learn one of the highest uses of our imagination. It is available as a launching pad, a portal to expanded perspective and, in our case the Akashic perspective. Remember, you can only imagine what is already within you. This is your personal highway to higher wisdom.

Now, imagine a lifetime in which you had tremendous wealth bestowed on you by virtue of your royal birth, and you totally enjoyed it! Let it go. Recall a lifetime in which you had great wealth by virtue of your royal birth, and it was a terrible burden to you. Let it go. Bring to mind a life of being born into dire poverty, perhaps even in slavery or part of a caste system, and it did not bother you. Let it go. And now, a lifetime of being born into hopeless poverty, serfdom or slavery, where you suffered terrible self-loathing or deep resentment for the wealthy. Let it go. Recall a lifetime of working very hard to attain wealth and you were very pleased. And another lifetime of tireless effort to attain wealth but you were very unhappy.

- Focus your attention on a lifetime of dramatic swings in fortune, due to natural causes such as weather as a farmer, storms as a shipping magnet, and not be bothered.
- And another life of extreme swings in fortune, causing you profound emotional distress.
- Bring to mind a lifetime of resenting people with money, and glorifying poverty.
- And then a time of glamorizing people with money, and holding contempt for those in poverty.
- Imagine yourself in a lifetime of religious justification for wealth.
- Then another of religious justification for poverty.
- A lifetime of smug suffering due to lack of funds, but feeling

superior to others because you felt it was more spiritual to have inadequate resources.

- A lifetime of arrogance, due to being unnecessarily thrifty.
- A life of deliberate disregard and irresponsibility, with regard to money.
- A lifetime of unconscious self-neglect due to fears around money.
- A lifetime of unwillingness to use money to bring your Soul's Purposes to life.
- A lifetime of appropriate distribution of funds to insure your Soul's Purposes were brought to fruition.

Let this all go. Now, direct your attention to this lifetime. Take a moment to identify your dominant pattern with regard to money. Most of us have a combination of restriction and freedom, enough and not enough. Get a sense of what it would be for you if you had unlimited funds. What do you like about this? What do you dislike? Now, what would it be like for you if you had zero funds? What do you like about this and what do you dislike? Can you love and enjoy yourself if you do not achieve great wealth in this life? Can you love and enjoy yourself if you do achieve great wealth in this life? Looking over your life, can you see any connection between your Soul's Purposes and your cash flow? How much money do you need at this time to take the next step in bringing your Soul's Purposes to life? Excellent. Give yourself a moment to readjust to this day.

Close your Records using the Pathway Prayer Process© and reflect on what you are discovering.

After the Exercise

It's a tremendous relief that we are not required to be perfect to be well used by life. Life will put us to work, and graciously receive whatever we have to offer, even when we are burdened with character flaws. We need only be willing to participate while imperfect, and not allow our shortcomings to interfere with our actions (though sometimes they do slow us down).

Another consideration is this: we only allow ourselves to experience and express our Soul's Purposes if we are clear that it is safe, and in our best interest, to do so. Because we love ourselves, we never let our Soul's Purposes to come to fruition if we deem them dangerous. Working in the Akashic Records, we have an exceptional opportunity to take a look at some events from other incarnations that are still troubling us. When they are bothersome, they get in the way of bringing forth our dreams. In our next exercise, we will have a good chance to observe what's transpired during other times and places, and how they're impacting us today. Remember, our intention is acceptance, no need to try to change who we were, what we believed or did. Just look for all the valid reasons for your behaviors.

Exercise: Your Well-Deserved Liberation

Open your Records using the Pathway Prayer Process©.

Consciously connect with your sacred space—that sanctuary where it is safe for you to explore your innermost truths. Let's begin by inviting awareness of a lifetime when you had strong desires to manifest your Soul's Purposes, but were severely restricted or totally stopped. Get a sense of who you were, what was going on and why you were thwarted. As you lived through this lifetime, how did you explain this conflict to yourself? How did you live with this limitation? By the end of this life, what were your thoughts about manifesting your Soul's Purposes? Let this memory go.

Now, bring to mind another incarnation, when you were active and successful in squashing the manifestation of others. Again, get a sense of who you were, approximately when and where, and what was going on. You would only restrict others if you believed it was the right thing to do. So, what convinced you it was best if you could prevent people from manifesting their desires? Release this memory. Just let it go.

Next, identify a lifetime when you successfully demonstrated your Soul's Purposes, and then you were somehow punished. Let's get a sense of who you were, about when and where. What were you manifesting, and how were you punished? How did you explain this situation to yourself? Let this go.

Allow yourself to recall another lifetime where you had a particularly positive experience of manifesting. What was the nature of your manifestation? What happened that made this so positive for you? Were you the only one, or were others having a similar experience? How did you explain this occurrence to yourself? What did you believe that made it possible for you to enjoy such a positive experience? Based on this favorable experience, what decisions did you make about the value of manifesting your Soul's Purposes? What decisions did you make about yourself? Now let this go. It will dissolve simply by ignoring it.

How about a lifetime when you actively encouraged others to seek and initiate the process of bringing their Soul's Purposes to life. Who were you? When? Where? Why? What did you know about manifesting or believe to be true—whether about people or manifestation—what convictions did you have that made it natural for you to empower manifestation in others? How did that lifetime turn out for you? Release this memory. This is a good time to scan the evolution of your relationship/your understanding of manifestation over the span of your soul's journey. Which ideas are most influential in this life? How much manifestation are you really comfortable with at this point in your life? Let this all go. Take a deep breath, and return your attention to the present.

Close your Records using the Prayer.

After the Exercise

When we do these exercises, you'll notice that we are not doing anything to the ideals and actions we don't like. Some of us have become accustomed to trying to alter what has been, refashioning our behavior, or results we produced. In this work, we don't engage. It's helpful to observe, describe and accept things to be just the way they are. And as we turn our energies and attention to other matters, behaviors and consequences preferred, the old ideas wither away from lack of attention. They shrivel up, and die a natural death. This is an aspect of the Law of Attraction, an influential idea lately. In its most basic form, it tells us that our attention is life giving and our neglect of any idea results in its demise. In the light of truth and compassion, it's unnecessary to interact with crumbling structures, better to observe, describe and depart. Your lack of attention will hasten their disappearance.

In spiritual circles, we frequently talk about "co-creation," implying that we humans are partnering with some spiritual forces to improve the quality of our existence. It's a powerful understanding which, when correctly understood, can inspire us to ever increasing positive actions and results. As humans, we have many natural restrictions, not designed as retribution, but to carve out the particular path of opportunity. Spirit is invisible to the human eye, without form, and needs our mechanical gifts to become tangible in the world. A great arrangement for both parties.

With that, let's do another guided practice to clarify our roles and responsibilities as well as our privileges in this relationship.

Exercise: Enhance Your Co-Creative Partnership

Use the Pathway Prayer Process© to open your Akashic Records. Return to your comfortable, customary place in your sanctuary of reverence. Settle into that sacred space, where it is easier for you to become aware of the deep spiritual truths about yourself.

Of course, the ultimate reality and great light are present, even though you can't see with your human or spiritual eyes, but rather feel a concentration of loving attributes. Excellent. Now, bring to mind some of the ideas you have about your Soul's Purposes in this life. Make note of the most captivating possibilities. Notice which one is most inspiring to you at this time in your life. Describe this idea to yourself. Share the idea itself: what it is, as well as how you think you can accomplish it. Observe your emotions. Does describing this purpose generate your happiness? Excitement? Deep inner peace? What emotions are stimulated in you as you elaborate on this particular purpose of your Soul? In the conscious presence of this pure light, feel free to ask for insight, guidance or wisdom about your ideal. Perhaps your original idea needs to be modified. You'll know if you are uneasy with your concept. Inner peace is always available. When we are disturbed, it is an indication that our dreams need to be revised a bit. If necessary, what modifications will make this a fulfilling experience for you? Go ahead and adjust your idea until it feels like a perfect fit for you.

Now, invite insight and guidance about this purpose. Spiritual illumination surfaces through our own voice, thoughts and feelings. You may have a question to contemplate. Life wants to empower you to manifest your purposes—you came to this life to succeed. What suggestions come to mind? From this perspective, are you detecting any recommendations? This discussion is designed to help you explore a specific Soul's Purposes. Let yourself receive this type of assistance to understand the purpose and how to make it real.

At this point, let's invite clarification for the particular ways you can really expect help bringing your Soul's Purposes to life going forward. Since no outside entity will do it for us, nor give us supernatural powers or change our essential human makeup, what can you really expect to help you manifest your Soul's intentions? Spiritual light is pure love, with all its emotional, recognizable human characteristics, at the ready to encourage us. It is a dedicated resource so we can become the most loving, fulfilled version of ourselves. With honor for who we are as human beings, identifiable suggestions and recommendations are always within our capabilities.

If it ever seems like you are being encouraged to do things that are impossible, like spend money you don't have or deny yourself and your family their needs, simply say, "No," and ask again. When we are in the earlier stages of cultivating this connection, it's easy to be confused. Be sure you keep your good common sense close at hand when seeking spiritual counsel. Remember, you are an equal partner.

Now, let's find out what's expected of us to fulfill our Soul's mission. Maybe it's time to learn something new, take action or any number of activities. Since the spirit essence of life is without a body, you are necessary to make spiritual truth tangible here on earth. Do you have any sense of your part in this? By now, you have a better sense of your co-creative connection with Ultimate Reality. Together, the rich, spiritual wisdom and compassion living in you can be delivered to the world in ways that are meaningful and satisfying to you, and everyone you encounter.

And so, for now, we leave this be and return to your place. Close your Records following the instructions.

After the Exercise

As we strengthen our co-creative connection with spiritual wisdom and compassion, we can find ourselves applying archaic standards to this contemporary relationship. For ages, we humans have taken every spiritual suggestion as command, and recommendation as imperative sometimes, causing harm to ourselves or those we love. In times past, we were conditioned to respond in these ways, because we were convinced that our value was questionable at best.

One of the most exciting features of this new age spiritual awareness is that we are a vital component in the equation of life. Our human self is required for the conscious transmission of love here on earth. So, if ever in your spiritual explorations you are encouraged to take an action disturbing to you, just say, "No thank you." Ask for another idea. There is no spiritual presence anywhere that wants to hurt us. But when we are growing into these relationships, we have to learn how to communicate, how to both listen and speak. Thank goodness the age of glamorizing false pride is over! Stand tall in the truth. While you may not be god of the universe, you are certainly the boss of yourself, and have the ability to make good choices.

We've already mentioned that Inspired Manifesting occurs here on earth, through us as humans, in time as we know it. It cannot and does not ever come into being outside of us, in unfamiliar locations, ignoring time. If something happens in a parallel universe, that's nice but not beneficial to us in the here and now. Observing natural growth patterns, we see that some conditions are fertile for manifesting, and others are not. In this segment, we take a look at some of the ordinary factors improving our ability to demonstrate our inner truth.

Paradoxically, in order to allow something to take form, we have to accept the world the way it is, without judgment. If I want to plant corn but live in the high desert, I'm going to have problems. To produce the heartiest crop, it's best to plant somewhere with rich, dark soil, plenty of sunshine and the right amount of rain. Iowa comes to mind. There's nothing wrong with corn or the high desert; both are fine. Iowa is not good for deep sea fishing or copper mining. It's wise to open our minds to recognize supportive environments for our preferred outcomes. We're always manifesting something, but our intention here is to generate more of what we want, and less of what we don't want.

Another important paradox is that we are challenged to stay grounded while raising our vibration. Let me explain. In order to be effective at anything here on earth, we must allow our physical world to be what it is, and ourselves to be who and what we are. As a short woman (5'2"), it would be ridiculous for me to shop at the "tall gal boutique." My opinions about height do not matter when selecting a good pair of pants. Noticing the presenting physical reality is a good idea. When the earthly situation is acknowledged, we are free to look beyond what may appear to be a limitation. When considering manifesting one of your desires, pay attention to the life you are living at this time. Your dream may require you to make changes, and be open to that or relinquish the desire.

Raising our Vibration

This is a curious concept because we cannot ever see vibration. We can however, get a sense of vibration through our emotions. At the most basic level, happy emotions are related to quickened vibrations, and depressed emotions correspond to slow vibrations. With us humans, what alters our vibrations is a change in our emotions. And, this is something we must do for ourselves. No other person can intervene to change our vibration. Some insist they can see and rearrange vibration, but that is nonsense. The best way to accelerate vibration is by finding ways to be happier, in this very moment. As we engage in thoughts and activities that are satisfying and pleasing to us, our vibrations naturally rise. It is entirely possible to be very happy, deeply satisfied and fulfilled while accepting our human situation. This is fertile soil for the growth of our sacred dreams.

With this understanding, it's manageable to elevate our vibration. But in the ordinary world, it is meaningless. Do your best to encourage positive emotions for yourself. Use insightful, loving words, invigorating ideas, exercise, activities with others you enjoy, pets, and the list goes on. Employing both inner and outer aspects of the happiness equation will naturally uplift your spirits, foster your well-being and encourage others.

Now let's direct our attention to another piece of our puzzle, the exciting possibility of supercharging our manifesting.

14

Supercharging Inspired Manifesting

Let's meet two powerful allies for conscious manifesting: acceptance and service. Both are vital to the process of transformation. Together, they represent both the inner and outer aspects required for Inspired Manifestation. You probably recall that acceptance provides emotional safety for us humans, allowing for unhindered development of new ideas. Service is the action element. It is through service that we activate the infinite, eternal love within and the mode of service provides for our unique individuality. Lucky for us, we are here in the new age when standards for service are radically different than they have been for ages. When we engage in service it must nurture and sustain us while we participate, engage and contribute in the world. Together, acceptance and service are a formidable pair, making our Inspired Manifestation authentic and valuable for everyone involved.

Acceptance

Recognizing and allowing the existence of something without need for approval is Acceptance. In many situations, we accept even though we do not prefer, much less enjoy them. For example, I accept the fact that my parents are deceased, even though I would prefer that they be alive. I accept that my sister no longer celebrates holidays with me and my siblings, even though I do not understand her estrangement. Acceptance is recognizing and allowing all people and circumstances to be exactly as they are, without attempting to change, improve or correct them in any way. When we do not accept someone or something, and instead assign negative judgment, the very target of our negativity sticks like glue, holding us hostage to a pattern of limitation. Negativity stalls the ebb and flow of life, blocking the passage for growth. Until negative pronouncements shift, energy fails to flow. In other words, until we accept everything as is, we are doomed to a certain kind of paralysis.

To accept, all we have to do is recognize and allow the presenting condition to be exactly as it is. Acceptance facilitates release and freedom. Condemnation results in staying stuck. When faced with an undesirable situation, consider it as an opportunity to love unconditionally. When unpleasantness, hardship or any kind of physical, financial or relational problem arises, ask yourself, "Can I love myself even though? Can I love myself even though I'm so judgmental and want to change this person?" I have found this approach to be the most powerful healing accelerator. Taking your attention off judgment and getting curious releases negativity's stranglehold.

Acceptance in Action

I recently met with a woman still deeply impacted by the sexual violation she endured as a young child, an awareness that arose shortly after the death of the perpetrator. Of course, she was upset about the abuse—and even more troubled by her own inability to prevent it. There seemed to be no way to offer her any relief from self-condemnation. It was easier for her to be furious (since she despises victims) than to accept the fact that her childhood self was unable to stop this horrible transgression. Her question to me as her Akashic Records practitioner was what she had done in a past life to merit such abuse. Working in her Records turned her perspective upside down.

The purpose of the Soul's journey as a human being is to provide us opportunities to love unconditionally, just as life loves us. Finding a deeper truth— that we are perfect souls experiencing imperfect human forms—we began to see that her opportunity was to identify, recognize and relate to herself with the same unconditional love that life has for her. So, the question to my client became clear: "Can you love yourself even though you were unable to stop this horrific violation ... even though you were victimized... even though the situation had profound implications on your growth and development?" "Yes," was her eventual reply.

Service

Another powerful ally in Inspired Manifesting is Service. When I feel like I'm in a funk and have lost my way, nothing moves me into the flow of life faster than Service. In fact, I've learned that the only way that life can get in is if I reach out. We now know that the chief opportunity of Destiny is to personally experience, express, and enjoy infinite love. This is most powerfully and quickly accomplished through service—giving to others in ways that are meaningful and fulfilling. To serve is to help, assist or attend. There's an important distinction here. Service is not unnecessary self-sacrifice, an old understanding of service, which usually results in martyrdom. From that place, we can expect harmful suffering in a number of forms. We have left the realm of martyrdom! In fact, it is radically empowering to reach out, inquire and act on behalf of the well-being of another being. This is the apex of service: trusting the goodness of life enough to set our own pain aside, and reach out to another in need.

In this new understanding of service, we recognize that true service nurtures both the giver and the receiver, and often sends ripples of energy to witnesses as well. Recall, we have left the region of dualism that includes "either/or" thinking. The old idea was that if I give to you, I will benefit, even if I dread the task, suffer beyond belief, depriving myself and my family of our rightful due. Going beyond the old idea, we expand the equation to include ourselves! Our new, empowering question is, "What and how can I give that nurtures and sustains me, as I give?" If I am giving while seething with resentment, I unwittingly poison the gifts! Better to graciously decline and offer what touches your own heart. If you love your contribution, it will be supercharged with positive attributes, blessing you and the receiver.

Importantly, service places us in the flow of mutual unconditional love within the web of life, where we experience the reality of our interconnectedness. Spiritual success recognizes service that is as meaningful and fulfilling for the giver as it is for the receiver. So the question becomes, "Given who I am, what can I do with what I have?" While this is a magnificently BIG idea, even the smallest of acts counts. As I engage in this inquiry, discover my own unique expression of Soul's Purposes in the world, I serve and as a result, my vibration shifts. This is the Divine Feminine at work: my internal, subjective, emotional sense of fulfillment that comes from service nurtures and sustains me. There is nothing more enlivening than unconditional self-love experienced and expressed through service!

Spiritual Success

Our next discussion is especially exciting because we have a chance to examine our customary human interpretations and experiences as illumined by spiritual light. We are more awake to our default settings with regard to money, and now ready to explore success and making conscious choices. Success is recognized as a favorable outcome, so it's personal, reflecting accumulation of wealth of every variety. Since each one of us has different standards, ideals and values, our definitions of success will naturally vary.

More important, however, is that we are considering "spiritual success" as an expression of love. When talking about spiritual success, we are referring to recognizing, experiencing, expressing and enjoying the infinite love within in ways that are meaningful and fulfilling to the giver. When contemplating spiritual success, the satisfaction of the giver becomes essential. As the giver, we always have the opportunity to be nurtured by sharing love, no matter what form it takes. This is a new idea, and quite powerful.

Historically, many would give to the point of exhaustion, self-depletion causing ourselves harm, unknowingly poisoning the receiver with our resentment. As our Soul makes its quest through a full spectrum of personalities, we know that at some time along the way, when our constitution bends in this direction coupled with religious and cultural standards, we may even be convinced of the nobility of excessive self-sacrifice or martyrdom. In authentic giving, the giver receives just as much, sometimes more than the receiver. Life is a dance of give and take, and we are learning how and what to give so that we are enriched by the act of extending ourselves. It really is a new age!

Releasing Old Views of Sacrifice

Sacrifice is also something to think about. It involves letting go of something precious in exchange for a better, more fulfilling option. In our contemporary understanding, we relinquish old ideas and behaviors, paving the way for more appropriate alternatives. One example is letting go of being happy to be happier. This is a bold transaction. We ask ourselves, "What action can I take that stimulates feeling love, and inspires me to actively share with others?"

Throughout the course of our lives, we've been continuously making choices influencing the quality of daily life. The time has arrived for us to be more awake and aware of our selections, understand and appreciate our motives and re- evaluate. Many of our decisions are still supportive but some are not, and now is the time to choose again. Even though we desperately want to make inspired selections, we may not know how. This is not a personal affront. Rather we are among the first generations in human evolution with the opportunity to choose.

Looking to our predecessors, parents, teachers, and the like, we may notice that they are equally in the dark about this process, no matter how significant the necessity or wish. We can cease belittling ourselves and others for making unsatisfying choices, and direct our energy to learning how to make invigorating, authentic selections. Let's look at some supportive assumptions, illuminating the role of fear and trust.

From a spiritual point of view, life is "for" us, as opposed to "against" us. This assumes that we humans are perfect at the level of the soul, while imperfect at the level of our humanity. In the light of truth, we are able to discern a deeper understanding: that life itself is designed to guide us into comprehensive, conscious recognition of our inherent goodness, the essential loving nature of all other humans and life itself. This is a tall order when considering the proliferation of human errors, confusion and chaos. Here, we detect a vital possibility. We are naturally paradoxical creatures, infinite souls in finite bodies, living in a world of restriction and limitation. Likely, our purpose is to find ways to experience and express love, to participate and contribute to the world in which we live, while we are currently imperfect human beings.

Consider that one of our Soul's Purposes is the discovery of how to engage with life, how to be useful even though our self-perception is that we are imperfect. This alters our direction a bit, as we begin to aim toward satisfying usefulness rather than perfection. When thinking of exceptional people throughout time, I have to admit that 100% of them were "imperfect," all with shortcomings and flaws. What's remarkable is that they were not stopped by their limitations. These are advanced consciousness, willing to share the best of their gifts while garden variety faulty humans. And, since it's possible for them—Monet, Virginia Woolf, Chekhov, and all the others—it's also available to us! So we can begin to raise a new question to ourselves: Am I willing to share myself while I am presently flawed? This is an essential question for successful Inspired Manifesting!

Benchmarks for empowering selections are simple, but not always easy. They require deep self-honesty, which is fortified by ever increasing kindness and respect for ourselves. As we become emotionally safe, compassionate and patient with ourselves, it becomes easier to be honest and direct. When facing a choice, we can ask ourselves, "Does this option give me energy? Am I excited, happy, invigorated just thinking about this possibility?" or "Does this idea exhaust me? Do I feel depleted and stressed out by the very thought of it?" And finally, "Do I feel more love/loving/loved as I venture out in this direction? Or less?" These elementary questions can bring our truth into focus very quickly.

Spiritual Significance of Fear

What about fear? Since we all have fear, there must be valid reasons for its presence. In the course of my life, I've tried to ignore, override, minimize and other strategies to get past fear. It finally occurred to me that it might be wise to examine the positive role fear plays in my decision making. So I began to regard my fears as my friends, not enemies, with excellent results. Here I realized that I am most afraid when insufficiently prepared. This simple awareness led to the next. When an option is not right for me, but good for people in a general way, it can be frightening. And, when the timing is off, too early or late for a particular action, fear surfaces again. All of these make it abundantly clear that fear is my friend, when I appreciate its good work on my behalf. The more I respect my fears, approaching them with curiosity instead of condemnation, the greater their value. Perhaps this will help you as much as it's helped me.

Trust is another area deserving our attention. In past times, I always wanted to have trust before taking an action or executing a plan. But it turns out that trust is earned through action. It's an "as" process. As I take one step into the unknown, as I experiment with a new approach, I begin to trust that everything will turn out as it will. The more often I act, the stronger the trust. The inverse is also true. Less action, stimulates fear and less trust, or trust in an unhappy consequence.

It's also important to recognize what I am trusting. If I am relying on my human self, alone, then it makes good sense to be afraid. As a mortal being, chances are very good that I'll make some mistakes. However, if my reliance is on the Ultimate Reality, or the light of Life, or God, well then, I can relax. Here we find another challenge. If my understanding of the light of Life or God is mean spirited, harsh, critical, punishing or any of those cruel profiles, it's a good idea to not trust! Who in their right mind would happily relinquish their well-being to a bully? No one! So, it's well worth my time to probe my honest beliefs about the qualities and characteristics of the god force. If the power of the universe is penalizing, then my fears are justified.

The good news here is that I am entitled to identify and describe the power of life in any way that I prefer. Why not imagine a loving, generous, supportive, merciful, compassionate, etc. Ultimate Reality? This is one of the greatest choices we have, the privilege of selecting our own interpretation of the Great Mystery. I encourage you to give yourself a spiritual partner worthy of your confidence. When we trust the power to be our ally, it is natural to trust. We can relax and proceed with bringing our dreams to life.

Making our way using a spiritual point of view empowers us to more easily release limiting ideas, feelings and patterns of behavior. As you would expect, this gives us a great deal more space to cultivate those insights, promptings and suggestions carried in our hearts to make Inspired Manifestation so much more accessible as we find our way to our fulfilling destiny. One of the basic Akashic assumptions is that everything we think and experience is somehow a portal to practice unconditional self-love. To release the negative hold of the past, look for all the ways you have been supported by it. Look to see how it is part of your ever- growing enrichment program for learning unconditional love for yourself—very decision guided by your deep desire to expand your experience of being loved, safe and appreciated in life. This spiritual, loving approach ignites release from the old and propels into an amazing life of promise. Acceptance, a baffling option at times, is rocket fuel for our growth and Inspired Manifestation.

Just a few more guidelines for inspired selections. Our experience of our process determines our experience of the outcome. The more we enjoy the effort necessary to bring our dream to fruition, the more fulfillment we will have with our completed desire. If miserable with the process, expect to be unhappy with the result. One of my favorite laws of life is this: It is impossible to suffer our way into happiness. We are invited to please ourselves into greater fulfillment. Another personal fave is that it is impossible to be satisfied with what we do not want, but we are always happy with our true desires. No matter how fancy, elegant, expensive, etc. something is, if we don't really want it, it won't be satisfying. This is so simple. And, honestly, none of us want everything, but we do desire some specific experiences.

When it comes to resources required for achieving our dreams, there is always enough for the next step. Sometimes we want it all up-front, before we begin, but life doesn't work that way. Our needs change, the world prepares new resources along the way. Don't be too worried if you don't have enough for the entire project, pay attention to what's necessary at this point in time, and you'll likely see that you have enough. Finally, action is almost magical. As we experiment and explore, the path expands to include ever increasing support whether people, ideas or material resources. Enjoy the magic!

15

Humility, Patience & Peace

Three additional elements can make a significant difference for us when manifesting: humility, patience and peace. Humility addresses being centered here on earth, patience is concerned with appropriate timing and peace is a quality of consciousness where "allowing" is paramount. Let's do an exercise to help us increase our awareness of our understanding of these very important allies to our manifesting. Acting before we are ready, we fall. Waiting too long, we miss opportunities. When we are patient, we give ourselves and our dreams a chance to fully develop. For us personally and the world, we are well-received. Our true purposes are valuable for us personally and the entire human family. It's a precise alignment. What you want to bring is exactly what life needs, at the correct time. Pay attention!

As energetic beings living in a world of limitless energetic vibration, it follows that our work is to expand our consciousness of these vibrations in order to manifest. Despite the popular phrase "raising your vibration," we do not raise or lower or control it. Rather, we bring our awareness to what is already existing. Importantly, the vibration or experience of peace is not "out there" but rather, already in me. My work is a spiritual realization of what is already peaceful.

While we cannot directly impact our energetic vibration, we have the ability to influence our emotional well-being, which naturally elevates our vibration. The highest vibration we experience is the joyful love of pure bliss. Although we may not sense it, we are swimming in a sea of limitless patience, peace, and love. Our work is raising our awareness.

Positive, loving emotions raise and accelerate vibration. Yet, the idea of vibration is meaningless for most humans because it is invisible and undetectable, except through our emotions. As we recognize, identify and experience our emotions, our vibration is altered. More love accelerates vibration into refined states. Less love slows vibration to a dense, thick depressed condition. Thinking about vibration is interesting, but doesn't affect its quality.

Allowing ourselves to feel our feelings is so important; personal awareness of our emotions stimulates us to continue on our journey. We go from being emotionally numb to awash with feelings. Because feelings are alive, they are always on the move. As we provide accepting, non-judgmental space to experience our feelings, they find their way through us, and beyond. Leaving us informed of our deeper inner truth and free of the messenger. When we deny our feelings, we imprison the sacred truth carrier. Allowing feelings whether comfortable or grim gives them the chance to move on. Feelings are not permanent; they visit, bless us with their wisdom and seek ways through and out of us. Becoming emotionally safe with ourselves through the spiritual practice of unconditional self-love is a wonderful gift only we can give ourselves.

Experiencing vibration is powerful when coupled with corresponding emotions. The way to experience vibration is by looking within and calling up positive feelings, (not sensations, but emotions). Focusing on these emotions makes it easier to feel them. They become real to us as we direct our attention to them. Allowing our attention to reside in the ocean of loving emotions—describing it, relishing, savoring and appreciating it, strengthens, empowers and intensifies it— and higher vibration ensues. If I focus on the phenomena of vibration, it becomes a mental exercise, which may be interesting, but is not very powerful or alive.

Pause to Reflect

Let's pause for a moment for you to feel into your current vibration, the condition of your emotional state and awareness. How does it feel to be in your body? See if you can sense the connection between a spiritual core of love and light and your Soul's Purposes. As I experience this, it's as if there are rays of light emanating from the central core of my being, radiating out through me to the people I love, experiences I cherish, places I treasure. Living at the core and within each atom of our being is the presence of love. Sometimes easy to access, other times more challenging. But, it is always there. There is an indestructible relationship between the presence of infinite love within and our Soul's Purposes. Catching a glimpse of our Soul's Purposes and moving into action, we unleash that fountain of eternal love we have been carrying since the beginning of time. As we're awakening in our spiritual awareness, we can effectively engage our inner wisdom to propel ourselves in the direction of experiencing and expressing our Soul's Purposes on the path of our ultimate destiny.

Some ordinary human questions help guide us along this dynamic, living process. Most simply, raising questions to ourselves about our human preferences in life, we find we are on the path of honoring our Soul's Purposes. So ask yourself some of these questions and let your answers be your guide.

At this time in life, what most inspires you? What ignites an experience of love within you? Are there particular actions or activities you do when you can really feel the love within you? What inspires you to express that love? What makes you want to take action on this love? What inspires you to express and share it? To ground this further, ask what makes you happy, pleased, inspired, content, hopeful, etc. Love is experienced and expressed in countless ways, find your most familiar combination of activities, people, and human opportunities that set off the feelings of joy for you at this time in your life.

Let's explore this in the Light of the Akasha. Open your Akashic Records for this next exercise.

Exercise: Elevate Your Vibration, Prepare to Receive Your Dream

Take a moment to consciously reconnect in your spiritual haven. It is your destiny to honor the true desires of your heart and now is an ideal time to prepare yourself. We begin by imagining. Let yourself sink into the Earth, to "decompose" so that the molecules of your body find their counterparts in the Earth. Here you connect with the elements that make up the planet. Give yourself a moment to rest, rejuvenate and then draw yourself up out of the earth, renewed and invigorated. Rise up. Feel yourself standing on the face of the earth as you are very much a part of it all and yet, a unique, individual expression of life. Be at peace with humility.

Now, turn your attention to your relationship with time in this life. Gathering some understanding of your general patterns with regard to time. Is time moving too fast for you? Too slow? Or, a combination? Changing in different circumstances? Are you normally patient? Or impatient? With regard to manifesting your Soul's Purposes, do you trust the natural growth process of your project? Do you believe you are an essential slice of life within the whole Universe? Does it make sense to you that your Soul's Purposes are important to the Universe? It is entirely possible that manifesting your dreams will take a long time. Is that ok with you? It is also entirely possible that manifesting your dreams will happen very quickly. Is that ok with you? This is a good time to open your heart to appreciate the ideal timing life has for you and your purposes.

At this time, in the richness of true humility, with respect for the reality of earthly time, open your awareness to the presence of peace. Peace is a fundamental quality of a spiritual atmosphere, and elemental in the essence of you. You are the only human being residing in the depths of your spiritual temple. Like the yolk in the egg, you rest in the field of the egg white. In your mind's eye, dissolve the boundary between yourself and a sacred environment. Let your inner peace flow out into the field of life, as it exists in the spiritual realm, and then flow into you. Be nurtured as you nurture. Unify with the power of peace both within and beyond you. It is your well-earned gift.

It's true that any one of us can be very gifted, or have an inspired idea to bring to the world, but harnessing our talents is extremely difficult in times of turmoil. The experience of peace prepares the way for the manifestation of innermost wisdom. Your personal peace powerfully prepares you to recognize and express your heartfelt dreams. Shine the light on your inner treasure trove. Look to see if you can identify one way to enrich your experience of inner peace.

And so for now, we leave this be. Open your eyes to the day at hand. Now take a few moments to read the Prayer to close your Records.

After the Exercise

Sometimes we find ourselves manifesting the same old situations over and over no matter how hard we try to do something different. Just as it can be helpful to re-pot a plant in more nutrient-dense soil or a larger pot with more space, it can be beneficial for us to change the environment in which we live. How can we become more humble, more patient, more peaceful? These qualities are like fertilizer for us on this quest, enriching our experience, enhancing our understanding and empowering our actions. Nonjudgmental awareness and acceptance of our present circumstances are ideal ingredients treating the soil of our consciousness so it generates more of the fundamental qualities accelerating our growth. As we adjust our emotional, conscious environment, our external world responds to fit our more current state.

Remember the Realm of Engagement? This is a space of human

connection and expression. In this space of awareness, our authentic desires combine with the world in which we live to produce something. Ever-increasing self-honesty delivers true desires of the heart, and acceptance of life, so that our cherished hopes can begin to take form. Our honesty and willingness to be vulnerable refine our objectives to their highest possible honor. Add an appropriate environment and the final result will be profoundly satisfying. By appropriate environment, we're talking about an optimal location for our particular intention. Some locations are better for our dreams than others. This is not a moral issue, simply a planetary reality. For example, if I want to be on an Olympic ski team, it would be wise to live in a place with snow and mountains, so I can cultivate my talents. If I want to be a television star, it would be wise to head to Los Angeles, or to New York City as a stage actor. If I want to be a YouTube sensation, my options multiply. Depending on the nature of my program, I can live anywhere I can get reliable internet.

I used to agree that people could perfect their gifts anywhere. As time passes, I've become clearer that our Soul's Purposes are not meant to be jammed down the throat of the human family. Nor should we expect the world to guess our dreams, or beg us to share. There is a relationship between us and the particular physical world we inhabit. As we do our part to adjust our thoughts and feelings, update our understanding, and take action, Life provides more suitable support so we can express our truth with greater dignity for everyone we serve.

Let's examine three qualities of consciousness—humility, patience and peace—to experience the best possible growth opportunities.

Humility

Humility, from the Latin word humilitas, means "from the earth." The process of manifestation requires that we are grounded here on the planet. The truth is that we are very much from the earth. Elementally speaking, we are composed of the very same elements as our home planet. Water makes up 70% of the Earth's surface, and also 70% of the human body. Six elements make up 99% of the human body, all formed in the Earth: oxygen, carbon, hydrogen, nitrogen, calcium and phosphorus. We are the same exact matter, albeit in a different form. We could be stars barreling through space, or people strolling through the mall.

Humility can also be understood as grounding oneself, which often comes from a place of knowing who we are, having a clear perspective—that we are infinite, eternal and immortal, and also mortal, finite and flawed. It is interesting that humility requires recognition, respect and appreciation for our real gifts, and also that we make good use of them. Being humble, we accurately understand that we have talents and abilities. We also realize that we are teachable and open to the reality that our abilities are not endless—we are not talented at everything. Humility is anchored in love and respect as opposed to humiliation, which is rooted in shame, and a searing sense of worthlessness. Humble people recognize that they are worthy, unique expressions of the Divine, swimming in an ocean of worthy, unique expressions of the Divine.

Because all human beings are composed of the exact same elements, we are all the same. Yet, we each have our own individual organization, which makes us unique. Unique souls with our own unique Soul's Purposes, none of us any greater or more special than any other. There are no duplicates. No one can take your place. They wouldn't be able to do it the way you would do it. I also want to distinguish unique from special, a popular concept here in the West. We love to treat our children as being special. The problem is that being special implies that we are better or worse than another. Therefore, it can be divisive. Specialness is hierarchical in nature, whereas uniqueness is democratic. With uniqueness, we are talking about individuals being made of the same elements and each of us (and our Soul's Purposes) being one of a kind over all of time. We are each the ideal, unique expression of our own Souls, which is distinct but never separate from the Universal Soul.

Patience

Practicing patience means being able to bear pain or trials without complaint. Having patience is the ability to remain calm, constant and steadfast as changes occur. The interesting thing about manifestation is that it happens within time and space, even though we have no control over the pace. While manifesting depends upon active decision-making—using our hearts, minds and will to move forward—once manifestation begins, the pacing is in the hands of destiny. We do not have control over the pace of life's creative processes. So we must be patient.

Think about the farmers who grow our food around the world. They practice patience, they trust in the process of life and they have exceptional willpower. Farmers have an inner strength to hold off planting this year's crops until the soil is just right, and the combination of environmental factors is in place. Their way of life relies upon a handful of fundamental decisions from season to season.

Practicing patience allows for a true relationship with time. It also requires preparation, setting aside enough time in the beginning to plan. If we have a dream of planting an herb garden, but do so before preparing the soil properly or before the risk of frost has passed, the seeds will fail to take root. If we start the seeds indoors too early, they will outgrow their small pots. If we wait too long to plant seeds outdoors, we will miss the opportunity entirely.

We can likely remember a time when we impatiently took our dreams out into the world "half-baked," and they were rejected or failed miserably. When we enter the manifestation process with patience and preparedness, we can make better decisions, and then make corrections when the results veer off in the wrong direction. Trust strengthens moment by moment. It really is the best possible use of our energy, focus, and attention—not to mention we'll enjoy a life of faith a lot more. In the absence of trust and patience, fear rules, creating an atmosphere of urgent rush, impatient worry or anxious hurry. Instead, patience keeps us open to the moment. In this natural relationship with time, openness naturally multiplies our opportunities, and amplifies empowerment.

Take a moment to consider a project you would like to manifest. What is your level of trust regarding this project? How patient are you to trust the natural life cycle process? Can you see that your Soul's Purpose is an integral part of the whole of life? It is both yours personally and also something that life is holding for you. As much as you want it, the Universe wants it even more. If you can be patient and allow your dreams to mature and grow, then your gifts will be well received. Those who resonate at your level of consciousness will find you. Those who do not, no matter how clear your communication or elegant your presentation, are not yours. Your opportunity is to pay attention to who responds positively to your offerings and who does not. When you receive your clue from the Universe... take it!

Peace

Allowing everyone and everything to be "as it is" is respectful acceptance— the peace required for manifestation. The more we can be at peace (free from fear and anger) the easier it will be to manifest. Peace is a condition of consciousness characterized by serenity and calm, an absence of tension or strife. At peace, we are free of judgment and in a stance of accepting and allowing. Peace is energetically neutral. There is no pushing or pulling as opposed to the magnetic nature of fear which pulls the object of its focus toward itself. Whatever we are afraid of, we attract, such is the paradox of fear. Anger is radiant, and it pushes things away.

When I am mad at someone, my anger alone pushes them away. Even if we are unaware, others can sense what we feel. They pick up our vibe—even when we don't. Peace is non-intrusive and non-invasive, neither insistent nor demanding. It is open, receptive, allowing and respectful. When we are at peace, our minds work well, our emotions find their own harmony and our ability to act is unhampered. When we are not being pushed or pulled in any way, we find our own natural trajectory, and are able to discover our footing and pace so that we can proceed in ways aligned with our desired result.

Exercise: Initiate Conscious Manifesting

Now let's turn our awareness inward using the Akashic Records. Open your Records using the Pathway Prayer Process©.

Settle into your sacred space, your sanctuary. The purpose of this co-creative relationship is to empower you to bring your Soul's Purposes to life, in this lifetime. While the spirit essence of life cannot "do it" for you, or interfere with the natural laws of planetary life, like gravity and time, expect to be assisted in understanding the most efficient, effective ways to experience your deepest desires in your lives.

At this time, take a moment to review "what" you hope to manifest (a spouse, a career, improved health) and describe to your innermost self what you hope to demonstrate. Let yourself tell the story of what you want—your dreams, hopes and wishes. Tell the story to that innermost presence, a dedicated listener. Next, consider the causes and conditions. Check to see if you are in a state of unconditional acceptance about yourself and your life. Notice what or who you want to change or fix.

Acceptance is the foundation of power manifesting. If necessary, imagine that you accept or allow your life exactly the way it is, as if it is meant to be this way for some reason you do not understand. Ask yourself, is it all right with me to be exactly the way I am right now? Is it okay with me to have my life be just the way it is at this point in time? Imagine that the way things are cannot change. Can you allow that to be the case? That's acceptance.

Now, given that you are a mere mortal living an ordinary human existence, what can you offer to others, to life, that ignites loving emotions within you? What activities can you participate in that strengthen your experience of love and goodness within yourself? True spiritual service nurtures the giver. What can you contribute, how can you give to others at this point in time, with the resources and skills you have today? What expressions of love can you extend that nurture and sustain you, providing you a way to enjoy all the love within you?

This is the dynamic duo for manifesting: acceptance and service. What can you do today that causes you to feel and enjoy the infinite love within you? In what ways can you extend yourself to others that unleashes the love within you, causing you to feel loved, enjoyed, inspired and fulfilled?

By now, you have a sense of some options for moving forward on your personal path. Considering the actions that seem appropriate right now, let's take a quick look to see if they are inspired for our ultimate good.

Does the very idea of these options give you energy? Or make you tired? Are you looking forward to taking these actions? Your human well-being and happiness are requirements for manifesting your destiny. And so, for now, we leave this be. You're doing a wonderful job. Give yourself a rest, and allow life to step in while you take a break. Be sure you close your Akashic Records using the Pathway Prayer Process©.

An Inspired Formula

Having arrived at this part of our process, you've covered a great expanse, and caught hold of many tidbits of truth about yourself. Significant spiritual persons are known for self-awareness and willingness to take responsibility. As we assume authority for ourselves, the light within shines out through and beyond us. It always surprises me to remember that the best way to intensify and share my inner light is by being a responsible person. We are on our way to Inspired Manifestation.

The formula for this condition of consciousness is as follows:

Human Desire + Talent + Skill + Action =
Inspired Manifestation

Four primary factors in our equation are rooted in our ordinary humanity. When we put them together, something remarkable occurs. That something is our humanity combining with grace, the light of life to bring about our illumined destiny. These factors occur through us, as us within ordinary time and place. And yet, the result is extraordinary. Examining this equation, it's obvious to note that when we are willing to honor the raw materials embedded within, and courageous enough to introduce our essential selves to the world, offering to participate, contribute and serve, something profound occurs. Life enters, and the mysterious magic of the life force co-mingles with our fundamental ingredients to deliver us to a magnificent destiny.

Destiny is from the root word, destination, which is the place of inevitable arrival. It's logical, the natural consequence of our awareness of our Soul's Purposes, our humanity and the life we are living. Our ultimate destination is a component of the "blueprint" of our Soul, living in the fabric of our essence as our complete, fulfilled potential. The destination determines our journey and, upon inner reflection, we grow in awareness of our unique possibilities waiting to be experienced and expressed. It is perfectly natural for us to grow into our destiny, because the seeds of our inevitable success are embedded within our essential nature. Destiny is never imposed upon us from our environment, but instead is revealed through us as our "emerging" truth.

We are able to stand in both spiritual and human dimensions of self, simultaneously increasing conscious awareness of the partnership between soul and human, here in the world, as if we have one foot in each. Initiating recognition of our destiny, activating all inner resources we need to achieve our dream. The core purpose of destiny is to personally experience and express through useful service to others the infinite love within in enjoyable, meaningful fulfilling ways. Our Soul's Purposes are avenues through which we have a direct experience of the unlimited love living within and, are so inspired by this reality, we are compelled to share it with others in ways that amplify our original experience of love. Soul's Purposes are the approach, the path, the way rather than the destination. Your Soul's Purposes are the spiritual essence of destiny/destination. They form the path of our ultimate destiny.

This raises the question: Can I live my life from the place of my purposes rather than move toward it as an achievable goal or acquisition? This exciting question puts us in direct contact with people, places, and circumstances empowering us to unleash the infinite love within for our own fulfillment and upliftment of others.

We've discussed manifesting our Soul's Purposes extensively, and certainly recognize that it is not a one-time event, nor is it a money-generating proposition. Because we are really alive, growing and changing, our manifestation will do the same. And, as is the nature of life, yesterday's manifestation is simply boring at best, and useless at most. Our opportunity is to be current with our manifestation, as it represents our present state of awareness, values and is our chance to ignite the love and happiness within. What thrills us today may be different from yesterday, and certainly tomorrow. Staying open is the key. As infinite beings, we are looking at perpetual manifestation. We are always bringing something to form, and we want to generate increasingly accurate expressions of our most authentic truth.

Perpetual manifestation is a fundamental condition of life. As we awaken, we strive to demonstrate ever more fulfilling manifestations. And in this atmosphere of perpetual change, we can discover for ourselves how to make changes without inflicting unnecessary trauma on ourselves or the people we love. This is a new probability for us humans. We endeavor to transform without adding unnecessary distress to a challenging process.

16

What Does Success Look Like?

Personal success is determined by each person, on their own behalf and on their own terms. There are many ways to define success, because it depends upon the unique combination of your gifts, talents, and abilities as well as the material reality in which you live. Success can be seen as the achievement of a desired condition or circumstance, a state of being or a physical item that provides meaning or fulfillment. Tremendous achievement without a sense of satisfaction (yes, even if it is $1 million!) is not a success. Happiness and well-being are essential components.

Your opinions about successfully manifesting your Soul's Purposes are the only opinions that matter. You decide what your success is. It's naturally based on your values, talents and evolves as you grow through life. Spiritual Law tells us we can only be successful if we recognize our desired outcome to be good for us, beneficial, fitting, correct, not harmful in any way. This is the end of self-sabotage. Consider it obsolete. Sabotage is simply evidence that we do not yet believe that what we want is actually beneficial for us; we worry it may be harmful. Self- sabotage is our way of protecting ourselves.

From a spiritual perspective, everything is part of a conspiracy, awakening us to our innate goodness. In fact, the word "conspire" means to breathe together. So, all of life is "breathing together for our support." Any mistake or perceived failure is simply another opportunity for us to love ourselves unconditionally to readjust our vision/dream or improve our skills. Our Soul's Purposes govern our path; they are not a mere destination.

Emotions infuse our actions and expressions of love. The next time you are cooking dinner, notice whether you feel love for the people you are feeding. As you prepare the food lovingly, it actually tastes better. But if you're riddled with resentment, the same food spoils with negativity. It's impossible to be resentful and successful at the same time. One supersedes the other. While the idea of success may be external, the experience of success is internal. If it does not meet your personal needs, it is not success. None of us can say for certain that another has achieved success. It is a personal, subjective determination.

Visionary inspiration is one of the wonderful benefits that come from conscious manifesting. However, it is important not to expect the fulfillment of an inspiring vision the instant it is identified. For example, I may have a powerful insight to write a book, but I can't expect to write the book the very same day I conceive of it, nor can I expect to possess every skill required to produce a book. I must do the work necessary, including developing the skills I need and engaging other resources to support my writing along the way. Life encourages cooperation, growth and learning. The need to develop new skills or request help for skills we do not have does not indicate failure, or signal that it's time to quit. Remember that this process of manifestation includes time and space to cultivate latent attributes, gather additional resources and activate potentials.

Every sound spiritual practice is built on an awareness that physical manifestation happens in planetary time, within the space of a person's lifetime. Physical laws of nature must be respected, such as gravity and linear time. When you face a limitation or find yourself overwhelmed by the possibilities, take a deep breath. Describe the desired dream, and ask for the very next best step. Life wants to work with us to manifest our precious contributions.

Inspired Manifestation is Not Easy!

Next, let's clear up an idea that stumped me for a long time. Somewhere along the line, I got the idea that an inspired project would come easily! This has absolutely not been my experience. In fact, I've grown accustomed to expecting that even my deepest desires can require quite an effort to produce. Any meaningful objective is worthy of our best effort. Attention, focus, dedication, commitment and action are natural requisites for manifestation. There is a vital distinction: when a project is my heart's deep desire, challenges do not feel torturous. Rather, they are deeply satisfying, enjoyable and even fun. It can be exhilarating to bring order to chaos or transform tragedy into beauty. Don't underestimate the invigorating possibilities of resolving problems, or opening doors that seem stuck. Grace, our mystical ally, guides and empowers us amidst the messiest parts of life. Relax, the life force is with you! One thousand mistakes cannot snuff out your light. In times of calamity, disaster or failure, know that the love within you cannot be extinguished.

Exploration and Experimentation are Essential

Although ours is a planet of action, all manifestation begins as a thought. While ideas precede action, there is no substitute for action. We must take action to discover if our ideas are beneficial, to experiment with modifications or improvements, and to explore the usefulness of what we bring to life. Usefulness, not perfection, is the key to success. While we may have a strong intuition, a natural knowing, we connect with the essence of an idea by applying it to our lives and observing the results. This is the only way we learn whether our ideas can grow and develop into even greater possibilities. That said, where did we ever get the idea that we must execute everything perfectly? How do we make room for mistakes and failures? Thriving manifestors are willing to experiment without guarantee. They have an attitude of "let's see what happens," and are willing to road test their ideas without worrying about what others will say, or how others will see them.

Ongoing Adjustments Accommodate Growth

Expect to make adjustments and modifications. What facilitates transformational change is our constant re-evaluation and re-adjustment. As we continuously modify, we expand our awareness, attune to life, harmonize and transform into our maximum potential. Life is alive. We come to know our Soul's Purposes by our feelings of aliveness. Manifestation is an ongoing process that is underway when we arrive on this planet, and which will continue long past our departure. As we step into the flow of life, it takes us where it will. Our opportunity is to allow ourselves to be transformed by our experiences. It's far easier to open up to life by surrendering. This is ultimately how we find our highest and best good.

This work is beyond self-development, self-management or self-care. Soul's Purposes stimulate our personal experience of the infinite love within us, and inspire us to express and enjoy. There is something so compelling about our Soul's Purposes that we always find our way back to them. Whether what ignites that sense of unconditional love within you is baking bread, ice-skating, meditating, walking the dog or cleaning—enjoyment is your best clue!

17

Personal, Perpetual Transformation

The more I splash around in the waters of authentic conscious manifesting, the more I see that manifesting is not a singular event, and it is not the final word. Manifesting is an approach to life. The new edge of discovery, as I currently understand it, is to engage in the practice of consciously manifesting, which ignites personal, perpetual transformation. And I understand that this may sound as terrifying as Leon Trotsky's Permanent Revolution proposal, which resulted in his assassination. In a time of permanent war, however, doesn't permanent revolution sound better?

We are Finite and Infinite

Because we are spiritual beings, our Soul-level opportunity is to discover how to initiate, experience, express, and enjoy the endless process of transformation that is the nature of our Universe. It seems simple and occurs naturally, but here's the catch: We are infinite eternal souls and, at the same time, finite beings here on Earth. Human

being-ness is a state that comes with limitations, including our unde-
niable mortality, endless inevitable flaws and unavoidable imperfections. Despite living in a Universe where the only constant is change,
and at a time ripe for an epoch shift, the strongest force is homeostasis.
We are embodied beings who much prefer the same old, same old to
any kind of transformative change.

The Evolution of Human Consciousness

Previously, our awareness was limited to our physical, material existence. We are among the first secular people becoming aware of our
infinite nature. Sure, there have been exceptions like the great Avatars
(Jesus, Mohammed, Moses, Buddha, Lao Tzu, Quan Yin and Confu-
cius) as well as the silent saints and monks who lived expressing and
teaching the truth of limitlessness). Now, it is our turn. Ordinary folks
like you and me are awakening in record-breaking numbers, on every
continent. As the light of inner spiritual awareness illuminates our
consciousness, we begin to recognize the love and light within ourselves, and within every part of creation. We maintain this expanding
awareness with spiritual practices, which experience is amplified when
done in the collective, where two or more gather in conscious intention and shared purpose.

Congregating in groups with like-minded folks is an ancient
practice. Our associations based on sharing spiritual awareness (rather
than bloodlines, geography, politics, race, or gender) are now forming
organically, arising from a recognized need or shared desire, acceler-
ated in part because of the world wide web. Members of spirituality
groups self-select; people participate based on their own personal vo-
lition (will). Contrast this with the religious congregation many of us
were required to join because of the family we were born into, rarely
questioning the tenets of the beliefs handed to us. Historically, decisions like this were made by the male head of the family, motivated by
a survival need for belonging to a community. Often such family based
spiritual affiliations stayed the same for generations.

Those of us engaged in awakening spiritual awareness came to Earth at this particular time so we can actively participate in this transformation for ourselves and the good of the entire human family. The collective leap will come about as we each contribute our Soul's Purposes to the global wave of Universal Purpose. The transformative change we seek will fundamentally alter our nature. As transformers (people engaged in transformation), we shift our energetic vibrations from one state to another by consciously, responsibly, and deliberately modifying or directing our thoughts, feelings, and urges to act to something other than their habitual object. As a result, we raise the energetic vibration to reflect the new level of consciousness.

Purposeful, Tumultuous Transformation

Transformation is not a singular event but an ongoing process. While most of us appreciate the value of growth, few relish the actual experience. The process of change can be terribly uncomfortable, whether rapid-fire fresh awareness stimulating new behaviors or long slow, deliberate, systematic adjustments. Change itself can be traumatic, which raises a critical question: How do I perpetually transform without generating turmoil? Actually, it's impossible to move from one state of awareness to another without any disturbance. In fact, turbulence is necessary to break up old ideas and behaviors. Jostling is required to disrupt old patterns of behavior. Consider ice converting to steam. Because of the application of heat, the atoms accelerate, breaking up their slow, solid pattern, eventually thrashing around to find their freedom, released as steam.

Turmoil generated for transformation is useful, even purposeful. Let's consider environmental activist Greta Thunberg. This teenage movement-maker is quite at home in the paradox of oneness, which drives her vision, and her own unique expression. Standing in the reality of her broken heart about the climate crisis with a wide-eyed clarity, she is passionately generating turmoil around the globe. Her Soul's Purposes recently sparked a worldwide Climate Strike. This is necessary turbulence to bring about the needed transformation, as opposed to unproductive temper tantrums we see too often on the world stage. The latter are useless distractions in service solely of the fearful, narcissistic individuals causing them, and thus, they result in no change. Growth does not come from purposeless chaos.

Neither will narcissism (the bastardization of self-love) result in transformation. Fear only generates distress, no matter what mask it may be wearing. Self-love is required for perpetual transformation. Conscious manifesting is self-love in action!

We each have within us all that we need to manifest our Soul's Purposes and to fulfill our destiny. Each individual embarking on this spiritual quest can cause a shift in the collective consciousness. In fact, it is energetically impossible to facilitate change outside of ourselves. Manifestation happens through us. I must do my inner work, you must do yours. Only by embracing our own inner transformation will the whole of humanity shift. As we transform, our physical lives will change to reflect the new level of awareness. Our Universe is composed of billions of individuals, each possessing transformational power. As we individually activate our own seeds of Divine potential, love and light shine out into the world, making similar shifts easier for others. In doing so, we each add color, voice and warmth to the infinite, eternal tapestry of humanity, contributing to manifesting the collective dream: the ideal of unconditional love for every being.

We are infinite beings, with infinite potential. Now is the time for all of us to take on the perpetual practice of transformation. In fact, this is the lifetime we've been waiting for! As we allow and accept everything to be as it is, we position ourselves to bring forth all the dreams, hopes, intentions and desires we've been carrying in our hearts and souls for lifetimes. We need not wait any longer. This is our time to express the treasures within us that have been accumulating for lifetimes.

Exercise: Ignite Awareness of Your Destiny

What follows is a series of exercises. Take them one at a time. Make plenty of space in between for reflection and recording any insights. Enjoy them at your own pace! Open your Records using the Pathway Prayer Process©.

Close your eyes and open your awareness to the reality of your existence in the here and now. As we've been working together, you have put forth an amazing amount of energy to identify your Soul's Purposes, and understand how to bring them to life, how to manifest. Recall that our Soul's Purposes are spiritual—they are the physical, material expression of our core spiritual reality. Destiny is our inevitable destination. It is woven into our essential identity, just like seeds planted in our being, designed to come to fruition through us on our journey. Awareness of our destiny determines the quality of our journey. When we are accepting, the ride is smooth, even when effort is necessary. When we reject or try to avoid our logical place of arrival, we suffer. We are always in a state of conflict. Your awareness of your desire for your destination is the clue that you already have within you the ability to realize your dream.

Each of us has our own dreams, desires and destiny. Yet we share a core destiny: to know and love ourselves, and others, as we are known and loved by the Divine. One challenge many of us face is accepting the reality of our lives, not as a punishment but as a starting place. Now, the purposes of your soul are the ways in which you engage in the world to experience, express and enjoy the unconditional love within you.

Today, what can you do to unleash that love? Allow it to find its way through you so you can be satisfied in your life. What can you do to move yourself into life, your life? How can you conduct yourself to be more involved with the people you love? Let yourself become aware of one action you can take today that will stimulate your journey of manifesting more of what you really want, and less of what you don't want. And so, for now, we leave this be. This is your own sanctuary, always available whenever you choose to visit. It will be here when you are ready to return.

Close your Records.

Exercise: Manifesting Your Soul's Purposes

Open your Records. In the presence of conscious light, there is a knowing, a recognition of your sincere desire to manifest your loving Soul's Purposes in this life and to discover your personal path of destiny. Your desires are the clues to your destiny, your natural destination. Your Soul's Purposes are the approach, the path to your destination--the spiritual essence of your destiny. They work together as partners.

At this time, bring to mind your Soul's Purposes. What do you do, what actions do you take that cause you to experience, express and enjoy love in this life? Can you understand that this question can propel you on your life path, a journey of activating the infinite love within you, sharing that love with others and being deeply satisfied in the process, even when it gets difficult? Where will this path of awareness and action lead to? Continuing along this avenue of love and service, where are you likely to arrive? Let the light of Infinite Wisdom shine on you and be open to what's possible.

Can you get a sense of your Destiny in this life? What is the combination of your Soul's Purposes and your humanity that is carrying you through this life? Notice where it takes you. This changes our idea of Soul's Purposes. Consider that your awareness, experience and expression of your Soul's Purposes are leading you somewhere. It is not the destination, but the path to be travelled. Get a sense of what it could be like for you to live your life from the place of your Soul's Purposes, rather than considering them an achievable goal or acquisition.

Now, let's expand our understanding of manifesting. You as an infinite, eternal, immortal being are destined to be continually manifesting, throughout your entire life, with your Soul's Purposes as your guide. You are always in the process of demonstrating your Soul's Purposes. The greater your awareness of what ignites the experience of unconditional love within you, the stronger the experience becomes. And so, for now, we leave this and, together, we open our eyes and bring our attention to this day.

Close your Records.

Reflection: Perfect Manifesting in an Imperfect World

Open your Records. By now, you have a pretty good idea of some of your Soul's Purposes. Describe which is most important to you at this time. Bring to mind all the efforts you've invested in this project, all the learning, growing, time, money, etc. Now, recall a serious obstruction. It could be an individual who really does not want you involved in this, or a group that feels the same. Perhaps circumstances keep falling apart, unraveling or spinning out of control. Describe what happens: the behavior of others, what they do or don't do that interferes with your success. Describe what happens to you, how you react and the things you do to stop the problem. Notice, that even though it has not been clear sailing, you are still involved in manifesting this ideal.

Now, invite the light to shine on your deepest visionary insight into how you can keep going even if they never, ever stop their nonsense. Ask yourself: Am I willing to love myself even if this is not easy? Even if I face opposition? Excellent. Give yourself a warm reception, and readjust to this day.

Close your Records.

Reflection: Manifesting--Bring Your Soul's Purposes to Life!

Open your Records. Consciously re-connecting in the sacred sanctuary of your innermost self, let's take this opportunity to become aware of the fact that you are manifesting your Soul's Purposes right now. You are arriving at your destination. This is your destiny. Let yourself become aware of yourself as the intersecting zone of Heaven and earth. The person that you are is the result of an ever-expanding, ever-strengthening partnership between your soul and your human self. Your dedication and recognition of your multi-dimensional reality stimulates all the inner resources to actually bring your Soul's Purposes to life.

Get a sense of yourself as the human expression of your soul in partnership with the Divine. Your primary purpose is experiencing, expressing and enjoying the infinite love within while you are still in human form, igniting the unlimited light/love within you for your own well-being and the blessing of everyone you encounter.

Now, at this time, let's recall your more specific Soul's Purposes for this lifetime. What are the particular ways in which you actually experience love, express love and enjoy love? It's natural to be moved to tears, full of inspiration and gratitude as this awareness takes hold within you. As a visionary, you may have a magnificent sense of the ultimate good you are here to deliver. The greater challenge is manifesting this powerful truth in everyday life. Given the reality of human existence, you can only take one step at a time to unleash the experience and expression of love, and it needs to be something you can actually do today or in the coming week. It must be something you can do with what you have. What could be your next best action to ignite the love within you? As you consider your next appropriate action, how do you feel? What do you think? Will you really take the action?

Find a quiet place inside yourself, and let yourself become aware of the relationship between this idea/action, your Soul's Purposes and your destiny in this life. Any resources you require to perform this action are already available to you. If you have to go into debt, then scale back the action to something you can manage.

One idea, one action at a time, you are building a bridge of your Soul's Purposes to your destiny. Know that life loves you. As you do your part, as only you can, the world becomes a more loving place. And as we all engage in this process, the infinite love within us all is experienced, expressed and enjoyed. For this is the Divine Will for each and every member of creation: to discover the truth that you are loved beyond all measure, and are here to share that love in obvious ways so that together we all bask in the ocean of love and understanding, shining the light for our own continual illumination and so others can more easily find their way. And so, for now, we leave this be.

Close your Records.

Reflection: Ideal State Practice

Open your Records. Get centered. Open your attention to the infinite wisdom and compassion of the light. Let yourself become aware of your most honorable, trusted spiritual advisors, even though you cannot see them, you can get the feeling that they are close. When we talk about this kind of "feeling," we're talking about an emotion. Maybe when you're aware of the presence of your unseen spiritual support team, you feel safe or relaxed, quiet or peaceful, excited or enthusiastic.

When doing an exercise like this, all of these positive emotions signal a more conscious connection with this dimension. In their compassionate and patient company, describe your "ideal transformed, manifesting self." Identify the specific qualities, traits and characteristics you would be exhibiting. How do you see yourself in your ideal state? Imagine being this version of yourself already, even now. Were this true, what would you be doing with your time? Your resources? What would you relinquish or avoid? Were this transformation to suddenly occur, what changes would you make?

Reflecting on these possibilities, what is most inspiring? Compelling? Your opinion is the only one that matters in this exercise. What do you think? Your consciousness is real. Enjoy it. Open your eyes and return to the day.

Close your Records.

After the Exercise

We have now arrived at an exciting part of our amazing Akashic adventure! Plumbing the depths of our being on every conceivable level has created a clear space for co-creation. With a clear slate, we can move forward with our intention: Inspired Manifesting: Elevate your Energy and Ignite your Dreams.

Up until now, our focus has been two-fold: clarifying our Soul's Purposes for this lifetime, and clearing away everything interfering with our ability to realize the fundamental blueprint of our Soul, our destiny. Usually at this point in the process, students have a good sense of what will activate and unleash the infinite love within them, and see how they can share that with others in a way that is nurturing and supportive. In order to launch ourselves into the realization of our Soul's Purposes, it's helpful to first identify the game plan, everything from recognizing our dreams to developing solid, sound strategies for making the great leap to inspired.

18

Manifesting our Desires; Seven Steps to Spiritual Success

This is the part of our adventure where we turn our attention to what deeply satisfies you. Having moved through the material, completed the exercises, considered the issues and consequences, you are now ready to mine the Akashic Realm for possibilities! Let's address our personal dreams. For example, I love to bake. It makes me inexplicably happy. It is an enjoyable way for me to experience and express my Soul's Purposes: to live in love. Curiously, I don't like to cook, except I do make a delicious pork roast. When cooking, I'm nowhere as thrilled as when I'm baking. Life does not pass judgment on what people, place or activities unleash happiness within us. All activities are inherently spiritual, and have a role to play in this great cosmic drama. Let's do our best not to judge ourselves or anyone else for what empowers expressions of love.

Our engagement so far has been centered on work, money and creative expression. Inspired Manifestation is not limited to these matters, its application is wide open to our entire approach to living. In this chapter, I'll focus on three important categories in our ordinary lives: Love Life, Health & Well-Being and Spiritual Growth.

Earlier I introduced the Power Protocol for Inspired Manifesting (Story, Causes and Conditions and Soul-level Truth), which is the outline for our work in the Akashic Records. I highly recommend it for clearing away confusion, and to see yourself and your life circumstances through the Light of Akashic Wisdom. By now, you are likely familiar with how that procedure propels you deeper into vast, compassionate Akashic waters, and accelerates your growth and transformation. Because it's so significant, it bears repeating: Every decision you've ever made, every action you've taken, every choice you've ever made has been based on the indestructible love you have for yourself. It is a valiant effort to expand and enrich your experience of being loved, feeling safe and belonging here on earth.

When you are ready to turbocharge your life, begin with an idea of what you want. Your true desires are the greatest indicators of what's embedded in your Soul's blueprint. What do you deeply desire? A better love life? Healthier practices? A profound spiritual experience? Chances are that one thing has more urgency than the others, so start there. We'll explore each of these areas with an Akashic perspective based on Akashic assurances, then apply the Seven Steps to Spiritual Success, and finally, enjoy a guided Akashic Records practice. All of this will ensure my deep desires for you to experience well-deserved results!

Akashic Assurances

Having completed intensive examination and a review of our past and present interpretations of life, we stand at the precipice gazing out onto a clear vista. We are in a position to view ourselves and our lives through an Akashic lens. Looking through our Akashic Records without gross intrusions gives us a sense of the magnificent possibilities ahead. This Akashic lens has specific parameters supporting our perspective, so let's review what they are and the ways they guide our awareness. I like to think of these as Akashic assurances, principles or basic laws presented to us with great confidence, upon which we can always rely.

You probably recall that, from an Akashic perspective, the ultimate and universal purpose of the Soul's journey is to learn to know and unconditionally love the self, others and all of creation. Applying this Akashic assurance to our personal work equips us to consider our situation from an elevated, rarefied place. Whether facing challenges in intimate relationships, health or even our spiritual growth, the overarching question supporting our inquiry is, How do I love myself in the midst of this situation?

This question challenges us to set aside prejudices about ourselves and others, enabling us to recognize greater truths about every aspect of our circumstance. Our assumption is that nothing is against us; everything is for our ultimate benefit. This new point of view can instantly jar our old ideas out of center stage, and open us up to new vistas of awareness. We keep in mind that acceptance and appreciation propel us into realms of personal promise, and condemnation and negative judgment keep us stuck.

The next idea embedded in the first is that life is on our side. There is nothing against us in the universe. The old idea of challenges and hardships arising out of a need for justice, or to balance some karmic ledger is decidedly non-Akashic. The Akashic field is neutral and comprehensive; it neither imposes nor intrudes, but responds to our own consciousness. This dimension is composed of primary substance, which takes form in response to our thoughts and feelings. It is designed to support us in positive ways, so we can more easily identify our beliefs as they take shape before our very eyes. This field is loving and unsentimental, allowing, accepting and appreciative, all to support our relinquishing fears and limited perceptions, so we can open up to infinite compassion, wisdom and expression.

When questions of motives and human behavior come into question, the Akashic assurance is powerful and distinct. Here we are asked to consider that every human being without exception is good and loving at the core. And because of their inherent goodness, and as stewards of infinite love, every thought, feeling and action is an effort to expand their experience of being known and loved while in this life. Even when people demonstrate terrible behavior causing self-harm, or harm to others, the underlying motive is always that they are doing their utmost to enrich their conscious knowing of being loved and safe here on Earth. There is no such thing as malice or ill intent. While there are many errors and misunderstandings on the part of people all over the world, throughout time, there is no such thing as evil.

Asking new questions empowers a fresh perspective: What were the valid reasons I made the decisions that led me to this dilemma? In what ways were my choices the best possible selections at the time? Can I see that the decisions of others were their best attempt to strengthen their certainty of being loved and safe?

These are the general guidelines supporting our exploration of situations causing us distress. Know this: you love yourself now and have always loved yourself, as does every other person in existence. Everything you have ever done has been your very best attempt to enrich your confidence in being loved and belonging here in the world. This is also true of everyone else. There is no karmic ledger, no balance sheet. The Soul's journey as a human being is an ever-expanding adventure anchoring divine consciousness, unconditional love while in human form. This is our quest, which is designed for our success and fulfillment.

When considering some of the particular areas of Inspired Manifesting, we know that these Akashic assurances apply. Now let's turn to three of the most important areas of life and learn how to transform our manifesting from predictable to inspired. As we continue our exploring, we will use these

Seven Steps to Spiritual Success:

1. Awareness
2. Acceptance
3. Appreciation
4. Action
5. Assess
6. Adjust
7. Allow & Enjoy!

These will serve as the framework for our consideration of Inspired Manifesting in our ordinary lives, later on in this book. Here's what I have discovered about each of them, and how they work to transport us from where we are now to where we prefer to be.

1. Awareness. Awakening to our true desires activates our awareness. We notice what we want, and come into relationship with our desire. For some of us, awareness is a no-brainer—we've always known, even though we are yet to manifest. Others are clued-in to their authentic inklings as life unfolds. Or perhaps this inner dimension has been delayed by illness, trauma, addiction, or troubles demanding our attention. Until they calm down, we may not recognize dreams stored in our inner treasury. None of this is good or bad. In each lifetime we have the opportunity to travel a different path to our inner truth. All paths are valid. Whatever yours may be, go easy on yourself. Complete awareness is comprehensive, including two aspects: what we want, the object of our desire, and where we are in connection to that desire.

2. Acceptance is recognizing the presenting reality and allowing it to be exactly the way it is/not. This is especially powerful in our spiritual development because it conditions the energies for release, letting go, and relinquishing resistance to what exists. Acceptance does not require our favor or approval. Acceptance triggers the process of liberation from the object of its attention. Refusal to make peace with any presenting reality causes increased, stubborn attachment to the matter in question. When wrestling with acceptance, we are challenged to allow the world and all its inhabitants to be exactly the way they really are. We also have an opportunity to increase self-acceptance, to make peace with the situation and our part in it. As we do so, we find ourselves in the enchanted land of acceptance.

3. **Appreciation** can be a confusing concept, as it calls for fierce courage to shine spiritual light on ourselves and situation. Appreciation is identifying qualities within ourselves and our difficulties for which we are thankful. When we can identify, locate and name the valuable aspects of any hardship, we are on our way to appreciation. The spiritual point of view is that everyone is always doing their utmost to enhance their personal experience of love. Keeping this truth in mind (that everyone is pure at the level of motive, and all actions are designed to help the self well), presents a different picture. The more we can consider and cull the positive value of anything, the sooner we will find freedom. Appreciation is like rocket fuel, launching us into another realm of promise and hope. Like awareness and acceptance, appreciation must be comprehensive (involving all aspects of any issue) to supercharge our growth (ex. the people, choices, actions, consequences, self, others, long term impact, and the list goes on). Every factor is part of the appreciation package and once begun, it hastens all positive change in seemingly miraculous ways.

4. **Appropriate Action.** We live in a realm of action and physical expression. While it is essential to be aware, accepting and appreciative, these qualities of consciousness are not enough on their own. We are here to act. Not just any action, but some action that is an accurate expression of your truth. The idea is to take action that unleashes the unconditional love and happiness within, and fills your heart such that you are compelled to share it with the world. The idea is not to "get" something, or even to

"give" something, but rather to "be" something. As we are invigorated by our own being-ness, we naturally give to others. Giving without calculation to receive or elicit a favorable response, simply giving because we can't help ourselves.

5. **Assessment.** Once we take action, something changes. Something happens. Our task—our opportunity and responsibility—is to evaluate whether the action is bringing us closer to our dreams or farther away. This is a decision only we can make for ourselves, and an honor to be sure! You make the choice, you are the decider; what you think and feel matters. While others may have opinions, the person who matters most is you. So take a good look at what you've done, how it went and how you are affected. A bit of self-honesty and willingness to observe will go a long way to inform your next selection. Was it satisfying? Worth the effort? All stress and no return? Not invigorating enough? Only you know in your heart of hearts what is best for you. And, that, my friend, is a real gift.

6. **Adjustment.** The information collected in step 5, Assessment, provides you with enough information to make necessary corrections. Maybe you want to alter your dream a bit. Perhaps you recognize the need for a certain type of education or training. This is the part of the process where you make adjustments to the vision and the path so that it's achievable. Don't underestimate the power of planetary reality. It can make the difference between fulfillment and disappointment, success and failure. After considering your desire, the situation, and the world in which you find yourself, you can make whatever adjustments you like. Imagination is your friend, so let it go to work on your challenge and see if it can empower you in positive ways. It usually can!

7. **Allow and Enjoy!** I love this step! Now, that the process of fulfilling your dream is underway, you can step back and allow it to unfold. Whether bowing out to allow planted seeds necessary time and space to grow, or turning your thoughts to other matters while the cake is baking in the oven, this is a wonderful stage

of the process of Inspired Manifesting. The dream is underway, the foundation is solid, the next immediate segment of the path is clear, and we are on our way to becoming fulfilled, enriched and joyful human beings. This has been our Soul's intention for us all along.

Once you have set this mechanism for spiritual success in motion, you can always step back into the protocol and make revisions. Inspired Manifesting is not an event, it's an ongoing process, requiring our participation. So, go ahead and jump in! It's your life, it's your happiness, it's your Soul's Purposes, all of which have been designed for your uplift and fulfillment.

19

Inspired Manifesting & Relationships

"Love! Love! Love! Love is all you need!" —*The Beatles*

You know the song. Love is all we have; it's all we need. The longing for love is as old as time itself. Every cliché about love is based on truth. Arts and sciences are driven by love human love, familial love, love of country, love of self, love. In the course of my own life, I've had the privilege to be in an intimate relationship with my partner Lisa for 35 years. During this time, we have had so many insights and understandings about relationships, all contributing to a terrific journey.

All of the participants in my life have made immense contributions to my growth in many different ways, at various times along the way. In addition to Lisa, I have had the honor of co-parenting our son Michael, who is now well on his way into adulthood. We adopted him at birth, and have been astonished by the love ignited by his very presence. At 10 days old, we took him home from the hospital. I still recall the startling moment I looked into his eyes and thought, "Oh, my heavens, it's you!" The recognition was overwhelming.

I had a similar experience with Lisa. When we first met, I was overcome with questions that seemed illogical. "Where have you been? I've been waiting for you!" These things happen all the time with people—we are already and always related. A sense of knowing one another that transcends all time and space has touched every one of us, in ways personally meaningful.

Delving into the Akashic Records continuously, persistently and deliberately since 1994 has provided me decades of insights, guidance and wisdom about the spiritual nature of relationships with self, others and the world, all rooted in experiencing and expressing love—our shared Soul's Purpose. It is a fundamental fact that every human being is always involved in a search to expand and enrich our experience of love in all its forms. This is the governing principle of our motivations, decisions, choices, selections and consequent actions.

Holding ourselves in the light of the Akasha, it's easier to observe that the core of our being is love itself. It may feel empty or hollow at times, but that is not the greatest truth. The real, sustaining truth is that we are love itself. Our challenge is how we individually can experience and express the infinite love within. For many of us, this significant awareness alters our quest from looking for love to looking for people, places and things that activate the love we already have.

This can relieve us of a great pressure to find someone to love us, to give us something we feel we don't have, which is actually impossible. Energetically, others can only give us what we are able to provide for ourselves. It seems a bit unfair, but it's actually a great system. This way, we are never falsely indebted to any person outside of us. We're not really looking for someone to give us love, or someone we can give love to. Rather, we are actually searching for people who spark that eternal fountain of love already present within us, so that it springs forth through us and out into the world.

When considering our relationship with another, we often ask if they can give us what we need. This is a fair question, but not very inspiring. Better questions are, "Is it easier for me to love myself with this person in my life?" or "Is it easier for me to enjoy myself and others with this person in my life?" I'm sure you can detect the shift from ordinary to inspired relationship.

Are You My Soulmate?

Now, the issue of soulmates is tremendous for spiritually awakening persons. From an Akashic point of view, a soulmate is a person empowering our awareness of our own Soul, activating the expansion of our Soul qualities of love, bringing about deep fulfillment and satisfaction with who we are and the life in which we find ourselves. Naturally, when soulmates uplift us in these ways, the best, most loving aspects of ourselves come alive. There are specific categories of soulmates: soul-growth mates and love-content mates being the most important.

Soul-growth mates are characterized by intense emotion, either comfortable or uncomfortable (like love/lust or hate/contempt). In this situation, the emotion is so compelling that the parties find themselves overcome, or even drowning in a sea of feelings. This tidal wave of emotion can drive the parties to disregard their good judgment, and take actions in the name of "surrender to love." While this is a popular relationship ideal, it is seldom sustainable. Its purpose is to shake us out of any complacency or emotional numbness, reminding us of the possibilities of relationships in this life.

Many recognize these soulmates from other times and places, and are convinced of the ultimate union in this lifetime, which is a very nice dream, but not the point. When this happens, by all means enjoy, but don't kid yourself that this is a long-term life mate. The person who can jar you awake may not be the one who can stay for the everydayness of life.

Love-content mates are those with whom we have easy connections. Yes, this is so wonderful and not dangerous to our inner structure, or disruptive to our life pattern. Love-content mate relationships are noted for their harmonious blend of soulful and human qualities. They are warm, stable, consistent, encouraging, and supportive of us, so we become our best selves in the world. In relationships founded on mutual respect and admiration, there is give and take, and a sense of shared experiences, both joyful and sorrowful. These are ideal life mates.

I've done so many readings for people consumed with finding a soulmate, someone they are inexplicably drawn to who is not available for a real life relationship for any number of valid reasons (they are already in a committed relationship with another person, an active addict of some sort or living in a distant land with no desire to move). With spiritually awakening people, I often see that they are able to recognize the goodness and potential in the soul of another, but forget to consider the level at which the human being is currently expressing. This is to say that they identify the highest truth of brilliance and light, but they may be deep in darkness and quite comfortable, unwilling to take the leap into the spiritual unknown. Here on earth, in order for a relationship to work, it must be both spiritual and earthly. If it's all planetary, it will be very stable, but dreadfully boring. If it's all spiritual, it will be inspiring, but impossible to plan dinner. When both spiritual and earthly are at work, both parties can be enlivened and supported in their everyday life.

Sometimes, people are grief stricken at their inability to attract a mate. Indeed, it can be sad. But, after looking into the Records of tens of thousands of souls over the years, I've come to recognize that we are in a new age of relationship. At this point in history, the purpose and nature of marriage is changing. For centuries, we have had arranged marriages, with zero choice for either party. We married for financial security and social stability.

Now, for the first time in history, we have the opportunity to choose our own mates in many cultures. Truth be told: we have no idea how to choose well. Our parents may or may not be able to assist us. Our friends are dealing with similar issues, so together we are the blind leading the blind, learning, sharing and growing every step of the way! Increasing numbers of us are excited to have a chance to get to know ourselves without a spouse or children. Many of us are exhausted from scores of lifetimes being married to people we didn't like very much, engaged in marriages of convenience, which resulted in domestic abuse. No wonder we are confused about relationships! By the way—we, too, are imperfect. I can certainly understand how painful it is to not get what you want in a mate. But, that brings up another issue. In the midst of this choice explosion, some of us forgot that all of us are imperfect. Our mates cannot be expected to be perfect or to meet our every need but, rather, the point is for them to inspire and assist us to grow into our best selves.

The ultimate purpose of intimate relationships is to assist us in loving unconditionally. Soulmates make that opportunity inescapable and, consequently, we fulfill our Soul's Purpose. Sometimes, when we find ourselves in partnerships with people who are caught in a cycle of harmful behavior, we try to change them. If it worked, I would encourage all attempts. It does not. In fact, this is a guaranteed path of failure. You are entitled to be who you are and so is everyone else. No other person needs or wants to be someone else's project. In a spiritual relationship, our work is to love ourselves in relationship with an imperfect human being. The point is not to love and forgive them—they have done nothing wrong. The point is to love yourself for loving someone who is on a very different path from you.

As we love ourselves and accept others, the world expands! We find it easier to be with people we already like and love, and to allow them to be with us. As an awakening spiritual being, you already know that the light shines brightly from the center of your being. Now, the opportunity is to know that the light that is your core is the same for everyone else. You do not have to attempt to give light to another. The light is essential goodness. Know that the light that's in you is also in every other person. Your challenge is to identify that light—no matter what the person is doing.

Safety in Relationships

Without a doubt, if you've sustained trauma in relationships, get good psychotherapeutic help. We live in a time when there are so many re-sources to support us. Don't deprive yourself, if that's what you need. The light is already there. But if you need some extra help, give it to yourself. You deserve it!

Many of us are concerned with establishing and maintaining good boundaries in relationships, which is a sound idea, to be sure. However, from an Akashic perspective, "boundaries" are a secondary issue. The primary issue is honesty. When we are honest with ourselves about our preferences and desires, and are able to communicate our truth to those with whom we are in a relationship, boundaries are not a problem. As we grow in honesty, the people around us either respond positively or negatively, and we have the incredible chance to observe the results of sharing our truth. If another person does not understand, accept or respect us, it is up to us to walk away and find another. Re-member, it is impossible to change anyone else. For full satisfaction in a relationship, we must feel safe enough to be honest.

As we grow in expressing our heartfelt truths, our relation-ships grow. If our relationship is threatened by our truth, it's the wrong person or the wrong time. Let go and move along!

None of us was sent to "save, fix or change" any other person. Our chance is to love, accept and enjoy another just the way they are in the moment. If we have an agenda to improve them, we are in deep trouble. That can be spiritually delusional. If you don't like someone the way they are, walk away. The world is full of wonderful people to love and enjoy. Nothing is more disempowering or discouraging than being with a person who wants to fix, save or change you. It's demean-ing, even if we have a hidden desire to be rescued, even if we hope someone notices that we are suffering, and we want them to feel sorry for us and save us. This is a faulty foundation for a good relationship.

In a true spiritual connection, each individual is aware that the other has the entire universe of light and goodness at their core. In a consciously spiritual relationship, each individual knows the other person is fine "as is," and has come into our life to enrich it, to share the journey and to help us learn to love ourselves and others unconditionally.

Relationship Challenges

Over the course of a lifetime, many things come to pass that can destabilize a relationship, from addictions to financial ruin to health collapse. Sometimes the relationships crash, and sometimes they survive. It's always the choice of the people involved, but it takes two to make a relationship. So, in the event that your mate leaves you for another, it matters not if you fast, pray and do sacred rituals to magnetize them back into your life. If they don't want to be with you, no amount of manipulation will work.

Here is the chance to honor the truth of another as we want our truth to be recognized and respected. Take people at their word. Trust that any actions another person takes are always for them, not against you. Assume that they are always doing their best to secure experiences of being loved and cared for. Sometimes, their choices cause harm to others, but their original intention is always to expand their own realm of being loved.

There is nothing to forgive. Choose acceptance rather than forgiveness. When we forgive, that implies that we judge the behavior of another to be wrong, and place ourselves in a superior position to determine the worthiness of that person. This is erroneous on many levels. We are not here to judge others, so there is no reason to forgive. If we can simply accept the reality that the other has made a choice in an effort to feel loved and valued, and their choice caused us harm, then we are free. And, they are free. Take off the judicial robes and work on accepting others for who they are, and who they are not.

When our relationships fall apart, as they sometimes do, we find a couple of great spiritual opportunities. First, we are challenged to love ourselves, even though we were unable to salvage a relationship, and are challenged to love ourselves even though we loved someone who was not perfect. At no point did any person ever try to hurt themselves or others. You selected this relationship because it was the very best option available to you at the time. And it was a highly desirable way to enrich your experience of being loved and cherished in the world. This is a wonderful thing to do for yourself, so be kind to yourself when things shift. Another matter to consider with respect to relationships is that we are living so much longer lives than in the past. Our relationships last decades upon decades, so no wonder many do not make the entire trek of a lifetime!

Inspired Manifesting and Relationships

Wherever you are on the journey with regard to relationships, consider applying these Seven Steps to Spiritual Success:

1. **Awareness.** Ask yourself what you really want at this point in your life, and be honest. Consider the relationship between what you want and what you have. Remember that you can only want what is yours to have. It's part of your Soul's blueprint to fulfill this desire, which is why you have the desire. It's an energetic impossibility to want something you can't have. In truth, we never want what is not ours.

2. **Acceptance.** Here our spiritual opportunity is to allow what exists to be exactly what it is, without additions or subtractions. We accept our desires and the reality of the distance between what we want and what we currently have. If we are currently in a relationship with someone who is not pleasing us, we accept that. If our mate is struggling, we accept that. If they are leaving us, we accept that. Acceptance does not imply approval, simply a recognition of what is happening, and letting it be what it is.

3. **Appreciation.** This is a real challenge at times, but can be so powerful. At this stage, we are invited to appreciate, cherish or value who we are being, and who we have been in our re-

lationships. We have conducted ourselves in specific ways out of the deep love we have for ourselves. All of our choices have been inspired by the love we already, and have always, had for ourselves. So the mates we selected throughout our lives were the best selections we could have made, and tell us a great deal about how much love we were able to accept at any given time in our lives. Extend some kindness to yourself for your relationship choices. You have been doing your best to secure experiences of love for yourself.

4. **Appropriate Action.** The more you actively appreciate yourself for your relationship decisions, the more you will enjoy them, and the faster you can let them go and make new choices. As you recognize the positive value of your past relationships, you will be able to set them aside and move on. Once this process is underway, you'll be able to let go of old ideas about yourself and others, and open up to new possibilities. Now, we have a chance to act in new ways, linking us to people who are a much better fit for us. One woman I know with a history of falling in love with active alcoholics (whom she felt needed her to rescue them) realized how frightened she was of being with a partner who was an equal adult. As she developed compassion for herself in this pattern, her need to seek out men who were falling down faded away. She started going to social events looking for men who did not need her. At first it was awkward, she had no idea who these men might be. But after a few uncomfortable gatherings, she began enjoying newfound freedom. A year of this practice led her to meeting the man who is now her husband. And, he is a fully functioning adult who she trusts with her life.

5. **Assessment.** Now, at this point, we take a breather to observe and evaluate our work. Is our action appropriate for us at this time? Does it bring us closer to our dream or farther away?

This is the time to notice and determine what is working, and what is not.

6. **Adjustment.** Simple enough—at this stage, we make adjustments. Perhaps we tweak our appropriate action or we realize what needs adjusting is our original desire. Maybe it was perfect in our early 20s, but is no longer such a great fit at age 60. This is your desire, your life, your Soul's Purposes. You are the boss, so feel free to make any necessary changes.

7. **Allow and Enjoy!** Ah, the best part of the process. Now is the time to let go and live it up! You are safe, you are love itself and you are in the flow of your magnificent destiny with all that love you've been carrying in your heart spilling out, flowing through you and out into the world. It's so potent that your dreams find you irresistible. Enjoy!

Now that we have applied an Akashic perspective and considered the Seven Steps to Spiritual Success with respect to relationships, let's do a guided practice in our Akashic Records to shine the Akashic Light on ourselves in connection with this sacred issue.

Exercise: Shine Akashic Light on Relationships

Open your Records using the Prayer. Let's take this opportunity to acclimate to the Akashic Atmosphere. Settle into the environment of kindness, respect, appreciation and serenity. Take a moment to identify some of the particular attributes you find here. In so doing, make room for yourself right in the heart of your own Records.

Open your awareness to the presence of your Masters, Teachers and Loved Ones, your spiritual support team, gathered because of their commitment to you, and your awakening spiritual awareness. While you never see them, you almost always get a sense of their presence and support for you.

Now, in their company, let's shine the Akashic Light on your current situation with regard to a love relationship.

Awareness. Notice what you would like, what you have, what's working and what's not working for you in this area. Describe what you feel is inadequate. And if you have a sense of what you would prefer, go ahead and identify your preference. Shine the Akashic Light on yourself, your desire, and the reality of your situation at this point in your life. Our intention at this step is to be awake and aware of the presenting reality of our dream, and the current state of our manifestation. This is not the time to judge or evaluate yourself or anyone else. It's only time to be aware, and describe.

Acceptance. This is a good time to invite the assistance of your Masters, Teachers and Loved Ones empowering you to accept whatever is happening. Now review your current relationship status, looking for those aspects which are satisfying and enriching, as well as those that are making you miserable. Shine the Akashic Light on this to more clearly see or sense the specific characteristics that nurture and sustain you. Then shine this light on those that drain and deplete. Notice that this is where you are at this time in your life. Ask your Masters, Teachers and Loved Ones to make it possible for you to recognize all the valid reasons you find yourself in this situation. Invite them to point out choices you've made, decisions and actions taken, that brought you to this place. More importantly, ask to be able to gain insight into your motives and intentions for these actions. This is a good time to ask to understand the ways in which you've been striving to expand your experience of love in this life. While you have some dreams currently on the back burner, let yourself examine the reality of where you are now, the others involved and how this has been so valuable to you as you are growing.

Appreciation. Take a deep breath and embrace the dedication of your Masters, Teachers and Loved Ones. They have been on your side since the inception of your soul, completely committed to your fulfillment, without reservation. We are now at the stage of Appreciation. It's difficult to appreciate anything when our feelings are hurt, or it seems that we'll never be satisfied. But, in order to fully release the past and all its patterns, we must be able to identify the positive value of everything and everyone in our life. With the help of your Masters, Teachers and Loved Ones, consider the significant contributions made to you through your mates. Notice how you've grown as a result of these important relationships. Look to see how your ability to love and care for yourself and others has expanded through these connections. Now, if someone has been a total jerk, don't pretend otherwise, but look to see how you grew through that experience nonetheless. It may have been a turning point for you, when you began to take yourself seriously and listen to your inner voice. As you extend understanding and compassion to yourself through all these circumstances, you will find yourself becoming free of limiting patterns, and welcomed into a realm of expanded self-expression.

Appropriate Action. At this time, ask your Masters, Teachers and Loved Ones to shine light on an action appropriate to express your highest truth, deepest desires and greatest hope at this time in your Soul's journey. The Records only suggest what is actually possible for you. Keep an open mind and heart. What could you possibly do in the very near future to move yourself in the direction of your most authentic desires? Let your spiritual advisors be your guide. You may wish to close your Records here and take the action. If so, notice your thoughts and feelings as you engage in this appropriate action. If not, let's continue to the next step.

Assess. Now, we look again to observe what happened. Notice what is occurring? What has transpired? What is stirring?

This is our chance to evaluate what is helpful and what is not. Ask your Masters, Teachers and Loved Ones to assist you in this assessment. Normally, they expect you to be the final vote, but are happy to lend their perspective.

Adjustment. Continuing on in our progression, we arrive at making adjustments, tangible changes to our dreams or specifics of our desires, standards or expectations. This is exciting because we are in a co-creative process with our Akashic Records, working in a dynamic relationship to customize our own heartfelt desires to an optimal fit at this time in our Soul's journey. Invite your Masters, Teachers and Loved Ones to be your partners in this adventure. They never impose or intrude, but are always at the ready when we call. Go ahead and make necessary adjustments.

Allow and Enjoy! This is the fun part of our process. Now that we've made our way through these steps, we can step back and let life take over. We are in good hands with a loving, generous Universe that conspires to bring us the best of everything. Be open. Watch and welcome your life as it appears.

Bring your attention back to the day. Let go and live your life. Know that you've set your course. Your Soul's Purposes have been recognized and validated through thoughtful response, feelings and appropriate actions. Get out of the way, and allow life to bring you the best of what you dream. Know this: as your ability to receive goodness expands, the quality of your relationships will naturally improve. Take your attention off others, and what you hope they will do for you. Instead, consider yourself and the next action you can take that stimulates that reservoir of infinite love living in your heart. Now, close your Akashic Records.

20

Inspired Manifesting & Your Health

Let's see how this all works when it comes to our health and well-being. Everyone alive embodies some level of health, or they would cease to exist. Since you're reading this, we can safely assume that you are healthy enough to engage. Our capacity for health has been developed over our lifetime. Whether we judge it to be fabulous or woefully inadequate does not matter. We are currently demonstrating a sufficiency of health based on our perceived needs and our Soul's Purposes.

Over the course of our many incarnations, we experience every possible iteration of health, with the ultimate purpose of learning to love ourselves unconditionally, no matter what limitations we encounter, or what world records we hold. From an Akashic perspective, our health conditions are not punishment for past life's crimes, nor do they come upon us due to luck, faulty thinking or bad acting. Looking through an Akashic lens, we clearly see that our current health is a very particular opportunity for us to love and respect ourselves unconditionally. And, this is a critical passage in the odyssey of our awakening spiritual awareness. This is how we see how our physical health and well-being relates to our Soul's Purposes.

When we take the long view of our lifetimes, it takes some of the pressure off of us to demonstrate Olympian quality health. Stepping back, it becomes apparent that over our lifetimes, we will certainly experience phases of exceptional physical mastery, as well as extreme limitation. Neither is good nor bad, right nor wrong, punishment or retribution. They are all simply experiences through which we have the opportunity to love, respect and appreciate ourselves unconditionally. When I first began recognizing this perspective, I was upset. I liked to think that I could neutralize my physical constitution, but this is not the case. The incredible spiritual passage from harsh judgment and criticism to love and respect is a beautiful and rigorous trek.

What is the Current State of Your Health and Well-being?

Consider your health. Most likely, there are aspects of your health that please you, and others that are not pleasing at all. Much of your physical health makeup is generated to support your Soul's Purposes in this lifetime. While I enjoy ice skating very much, I do not have the physical capacity for professional level skating, nor do I have the requisite interest in training or living the life of a serious athlete. How perfect! Because I can go and enjoy skating without any pressure, and also watch professional ice skaters with great admiration and appreciation.

Experiencing and expressing love through skating is not the dominant purpose of my Soul in this lifetime, and so my body is not equipped to deliver that level of expertise. My Soul's Purposes are in other areas, and my body is perfect for the work I do. I love to bike to work, and then sit and read and write and drink tea—all ideal physical traits for my Soul's Purposes.

Observing human life, I notice that some people are born with serious physical difficulties, and others are not. Some folks overcome their perceived imperfections, others do not. Everyone dies. Some die young, many die aged. Death is not an indictment or evidence of failure. It's a customary occurrence like birth. It's a passage from one state of being to another. Neither is better than another.

Certainly we enjoy stories of people who have overcome dreaded diseases, triumphed over physical limitations, or even used their impairments as a way to make a significant contribution to humanity. All of these are valid. But, it is also just as meaningful and valid to get sick and die, to suffer without relief, to chafe within the limits of a disability. Every health situation is an opportunity to love ourselves unconditionally, which sounds simple, but is not easy.

Considering our present state of health and well-being through an Akashic lens, the turbo charged healing questions become:

- *How do I love myself even though I'm sick and cannot seem to cure myself?*
- *How do I not use this as a weapon against myself?*
- *How do I love another even though they are sick and not getting better?*
- *How do I love others when they are suffering for extended periods of time?*
- *How do I love the people who care for them?*
- *How do I love myself even though I cannot cure the people I love of their ailments?*

These are truly spiritual questions that can accelerate our journey from detached, uncaring, critical and fearful to compassionate, caring, accepting and loving. These are the questions that define our quest. Our purpose is to connect with the love within, disconnect from judgment and allow ourselves to experience compassion and patience, even when we don't know what to do. We should stop expecting others to heal themselves. Maybe they will, and maybe they won't. Maybe this lifetime they are here to learn to love themselves despite "failing" to self- heal. We don't know.

Keep asking, "How do I love myself in the midst of the mystery of life? And how do I relinquish judgment and criticism of others when I don't know what to do?" This includes mental health as well. I am not a doctor and have no formal opinion about physical or mental health issues. But from a spiritual point of view, I see two important factors. First, the difference between a sophisticated spiritual awareness and mental illness is responsibility. A spiritual person without mental illness has the ability to direct their own thoughts. When a person is dealing with a mental illness, they do not have authority over their thinking. We live in wonderful times of excellent mental health practitioners who are trained to assist those in need. There is nothing spiritual about refusing necessary help. It's actually evidence of the depth of the need for such assistance.

Many people with mental health challenges are talented in a variety of ways, blessing those in their world. There are also many with these difficulties who are not so talented. Mental illness is neither a benefit or a detriment. It is an experience. The questions from an Akashic point of view become, "How do I love and respect myself when I have a mental illness? How do I love and respect myself when I am unable to cure someone I love from their mental health issues?" Again, the Soul is seeking experiences of unconditional love for self. Mental health issues are just another opportunity to expand our self-love and diminish judgment.

With all of this in mind, let's take a look at the Seven Steps to Spiritual Success with regard to our health:

Awareness. This is the time to take a good, clear-eyed look at the current state of your health, physical and mental. How are you doing? What's happening that brought this dimension of yourself to your attention? Is there a gap between how you feel and the state of health you would ideally like to have? At this stage, identify your presenting reality and any judgments you have about your current state of health. For me, I notice I am 65 years old. My health is very good but, honestly, I don't have the same amount of energy or endurance that I had at 35, much less firm stomach muscles. Is this a reason to be annoyed with myself?

No. It seems like whatever energy it would take to have a flat, firm stomach I simply do not have. Is this a reason to be irritated at myself? Do I think of these things as evidence of my spiritual inferiority? What's more, after 24 trips to Asia in 4 years, I find myself totally exhausted. When I found myself disappointed for being tired, a friend pointed out that jet lag is real and that I have been demanding a lot of my body, which has actually been quite supportive as I stretched it during this time. Now it's time to give it a rest. As I gave up my unrealistic ideas of what I "should" be able to do at this point in my life, I began resting more deeply, and finding restoration on every level.

Acceptance. This is the time to stop resisting what's really happening. Acceptance means recognizing the present reality of our situation. Awhile back, I awoke to find that my jeans no longer fit. At first, I wanted to believe that they shrunk, but that just wasn't true. I was overeating and not getting enough exercise. It was a rude reality, one I did not like one little bit. But, it was a turning point for me. I awoke to the new reality and made a decision to implement a few changes in my diet and exercise. Acceptance gave me the space to take new actions that brought me to a better place, one I happen to like much more. Was I spiritually inept because I gained weight? Was it wrong to make a deliberate decision and make some changes? The opportunity was to accept the new reality, whether I liked it or not. And once that acceptance registered within me, I was free to make new choices to support my Soul's Purposes. The question continues to be, "How do I love myself even though I gained some weight? Even though I need the support of a food plan and exercise?" Acceptance opens the space to make new choices more appropriate to our current needs.

Appreciation. Appreciation launches our transformation. We cannot be resistant and also appreciative. After the age of 60, I found myself with some unusual physical discomfort that I was unable to control with positive thinking, herbs or exercises. Visiting my regular doctor, I found myself with a prescription for medication for high blood pressure. Initially, I was very disappointed in myself, because I had believed I would be able to avoid all medical intervention. But here I was, being humbled by a condition that stalked my parents, grandparents, aunts, uncles, cousins and siblings, even causing blindness in one aunt. I did not want to be a victim of some family disease. Ah—the challenge! How do I love myself even though I inherited this same family disease? How do I love myself even though I'm just another mere mortal in the group? Oh, how my poor ego struggled with this. After a fruitless round of self-pity, I was struck with a new insight. It turns out that I was born during a time when medication is plentiful for this condition. I can actually take the medication without crippling side effects. With this, I began appreciating all the surrounding pieces of this situation until I came crashing into the matter of the high blood pressure itself. How can I appreciate having this? Now, I'm still in the process but can report that at this time, I am feeling grateful because it has become a powerful path of growing into increasing unconditional self-love. This has been an entirely new arena of expansion and, for that, I am appreciative. Energetically, appreciation serves as rocket fuel for manifesting. Try it!

Appropriate action. As already discussed, this is a planet of action! So, too, with our health, we need to consider what is appropriate action for us at this time. In the case of my high blood pressure, exercise is a big help. Not every exercise is helpful, but walking in particular is excellent for me. I used to look down on people who walked; I thought it was for weaklings and old people. Well, isn't that hilarious? I'm an old person and it's the perfect action to support my health. I once harbored dreams of running a marathon, but I am unwilling to do the work required to make it a reality. But I can walk miles and miles. It's easy, and I enjoy it. How do I love myself even though my best athletic effort is walking? Every element of this seven-stage process gives us a chance to release antiquated notions, and embrace ourselves just the way we are today.

Assessment. At this time in our process, we have the chance to observe and evaluate our progress. This is your journey and your life. Your opinion matters. So, ask yourself, how things are developing, and answer honestly. What's working? What's not working? These are foundational questions. You have a goal or ideal of the actions you're taking, and whether they are moving you closer to your ideal or further away. If you are drifting away, be especially kind to yourself. But ask, "How do I love myself even though my idea is not helpful? Or if you are having success ask, "How do I love myself when I am successful?" There is always a good reason to love and respect yourself more. This is an interesting stage of the process, because it gives us a chance to determine which actions are productive versus those that are not.

Adjustment. This is our opportunity to fine tune our process. During the adjustment phase, I can observe and make note of the results I'm producing, as well as considering whether they are helpful. If they are—then, awesome. If not, it's time to make some changes. Change is a given when we are involved in our own process. Often, we don't know for sure whether something will work until we actually do it. And once we take action, we gather so much information about ourselves and learn what supports us. Expect to make adjustments. Last year, we got a new puppy, an Irish Doodle we named Chadwick the Adorable. He is a love of a fella—and always in need of a walk. I feel as if life brought us together so that we can support one another in maintaining our well-being. Chadwick is absolutely the best walking buddy I could ever dream of! For a time, I was upset because I wanted a partner to walk. My question became, "How do I love myself even when I need a walking buddy?" As I let go of expectations for myself and softened my real needs, it all became so much easier—not to mention more fun. If you are being stubborn about any necessary adjustments you have to make, check your judgments. And then ask the $50 million question, "How do I love myself even though ...?" and more will be revealed to you!

Allow and Enjoy! Finally, we are at step 7. It's time to step back and let life take over. Allowing implies a positive trust in the goodness of life, trusting that we have done our best, working in a co-creative partnership with life. Now that we've done our part, we can safely relinquish the reins and let life lead the way. Enjoyment is naturally ours when we do. We are in the flow of experiencing, enhancing and enriching our unconditional self-love, and reaping some positive ordinary life benefits. What's not to enjoy? Maybe we achieve our dreams, maybe we don't, but the journey itself is nurturing and sustaining as we continue on our path.

Now that we have examined this in our ordinary state of awareness, let's shine Akashic Light on our health challenges, illuminating possibilities for our transformation and fulfillment. Even more exciting is the possibility that we will come face to face with the personal, spiritual realities of health.

Exercise: Your Health and Well-being

Open your Records using the Pathway Prayer Process©. Let yourself settle into the sacred sanctuary that is your Records. Extend your awareness so you can identify some of the most obvious qualities that you find in your Records. Normally, we find emotional warmth and welcome, graciousness and understanding, or some other qualities like these. Invite your Masters, Teachers and Loved Ones to give you the support you need to recognize the truths empowering you to grow in this area.

We begin with Awareness. Imagine you are having an important discussion with your most trusted advisors. Describe your current health situation, not just the label of diagnosis, but exploring what's happening or not. It may be a physical or mental health challenge. Describe what you are experiencing, along with how you understand it. In addition to your present difficulty, you likely have a desired or preferred health goal that is unattainable at this moment. Identify your preference. What do you want? Name it. Describe what you are hoping for. What is the gap between what you have, and what you want? Describe this as well.

Included in our Awareness stage, we shine the Akashic Light on our judgments, fears, worries, resentments, and all the emotions we have about this matter. This is very important, since transformation occurs through us, as the people we are. Holding steady in the Akashic Light with the assistance of our Masters, Teachers and Loved Ones, we look beyond what we already know and believe, we ask for support to grasp the ultimate truth of health as it is available to us personally. Stretch your awareness as much as you can to consider the possibility that impeccable health resides within you at this very moment, without consideration for your physical limitations, mental imperfections or emotional distress. Focus on the idea that optimal health is already a part of you, embedded as a spiritual essence within the core of your being. The health that comprises your essence is in no way crippled or corrupted; it is whole, vibrant, complete and effervescent. Let your awareness rest on this reality, the true spiritual reality.

At this point, understand that your human self is the vehicle through which this breathtaking energy travels from the center of your being, through you and into your world. This is the greatest truth. And, if your physical, emotional or mental expressions are constricted in some way, that does not indicate that the energy itself is damaged. It is energetically impossible to extinguish the health that is the core of you. Make room for this new awareness.

Next, we continue to Acceptance. It's critical to remember that this does not imply approval. We don't have to be happy with our situation. We only have to recognize the reality of our condition, and our response to it. Ask your Masters, Teachers and Loved Ones to shine Akashic Light on this matter of acceptance.

It's very common to have a surge of resistance when urged to accept something unpleasant. However, acceptance triggers release. So, if for no other reason than being supported, try accepting your situation. As you allow your expression of health to be exactly what it is at this time, without any criticism or judgment, any pent-up energies from a tense dynamic are diffused, and everything becomes less stuck. What constriction, confusion or restriction do you have at this time, and how is it preventing the easy, free flow of ultimate health? Just notice. Observe. Describe. Make notes. And accept. Accept that this is your best effort at this time. Accept that even though the flow of the life force has been slowed by your conditions, it has not stopped the flow. Accept that at some point in this lifetime, it was in your best interest to adopt these patterns of health. You took them on because they were a good idea, a sound idea at the time of adoption.

We are asked to accept a lot. It's wise to invite the support of our Masters, Teachers and Loved Ones so that we can amplify our ability to accept all facets of our relationship to health. Accept your customary level of health and well-being. Accept the judgments and criticisms you have of yourself, and any other people or institutions, such as doctors or other medical professionals. Accept the consequences of your circumstances. Ask, "How do I love myself even though...?" Don't worry about loving anyone else right now. That will come in time. For now, you're the one who needs your love and positive attention. Ask, "How do I love myself even though I am full of anger, self-pity (or any other unpleasant emotion attached to this matter)?" And now, we accept that perfect health and well-being already live within us. No need to do anything, just recognize this truth.

Now we proceed to Appreciation. This is so powerful. At this stage, we are asked to seek and find the personal, positive value of our situation. Here we take a moment to acknowledge ourselves for this creative way we've found to learn how to love ourselves unconditionally. We look to see the ways in which we've been empowered, taken good care of ourselves, because we have this condition.

Appreciate yourself for the kind and merciful ways you've allowed these concerns to carve your path, develop and utilize your gifts, talents and abilities. As we appreciate the benefits of our situation and the way we have been able to make good use of a tough challenge, negative energy drains out of us. We stop adding hostile attitudes and emotions to our already delicate conditions. This is a powerful step on the way to freedom from limiting patterns of ideas and actions. And it feels good, too. As we feel positive and loving toward ourselves, the distance between our current physical, emotional and mental well-being and expectations of optimal health diminishes. Let yourself appreciate yourself in this difficult situation.

It's time for Appropriate Action. In the reassuring company of your Masters, Teachers and Loved Ones, ask for suggestions about an action you can actually take that is appropriate for you in this specific situation. The guidance may come to you like a flash thought, a memory or a slow, steady realization. It may be in words or pictures. Don't concern yourself with the way it comes to your attention. All are valid. As it comes to your attention, describe what the action seems like. What's involved, and necessary for you to do to perform? This is a time to bring your good common sense into your spiritual practice, and look for the sound reasons this action will support you at this time. If it does not make sense to you, don't do it! Keep looking around for a positive, appropriate action you can take to move yourself closer to your ideal.

When we receive guidance about an appropriate action, it will be manageable, supportive and immediate, or doable in the next few days. If it's overwhelming, or seems like it will cause problems, then it's probably not from the Records. The Records never urge us to take any action that will cause harm to us or any other person—no financial harm, no physical, emotional or mental damage.

With the guiding presence of your Masters, Teachers and Loved Ones in a co- creative partnership, the recommendations coming to your attention will be within your reach, and always moving you closer to your ideal health. While you already have ultimate health within, your human self may not be in a condition to allow maximum health to transmit at this time. Once again, this raises the turbo-charged healing question, "How do I love myself when I am so far away from my desire for optimal health?"

Assessment is the next step in our progression. Having taken appropriate action, we have some new information about ourselves, our dreams and the world in which we live. In the co-creative partnership with your Masters, Teachers and Loved Ones, describe the status of your health, your desires and your awareness of the presence of ultimate health as a spiritual resource living within you. Notice the action you took in the last step and observe the results. Were they positive? Negative? Did they have mixed consequences? With this new information you have a chance to determine what is still valid and fitting for you. In a perfect world without judgment, how would you assess this situation? If you were certain of resounding success at some point in the process, what would you allow yourself to recognize? Naturally, this is another great opportunity to ask yourself the super-charged healing question, "How do I love myself when I notice some changes are required?"

Take a deep breath now, as we continue to our next step of Adjustment. Now is the time to make some alterations, adjustments in some part of your understanding, solution, or dream. Let your Masters, Teachers and Loved Ones help you with this. Ask them to shine the Akashic Light on the state of the union with your health, and ask for guidance about what changes need to be made. Some may be very clear to you without spiritual support, others may require some extra insight, guidance and wisdom. Keep an open mind. Any adjustments will give you a sense of relief, and hasten your journey to fulfillment.

Understand that impeccable health is the core of your being. Necessary adjustments will move you closer to this infinite reservoir of love, and empower satisfaction. If you find yourself feeling frightened or stubborn, ask for assistance. And don't forget the turbo-charged healing question, "How do I love and respect myself even though I need to make changes?"

This protocol delivers us to the seventh and final stage of the process—*Allow and Enjoy!* With the reassurance of your Masters, Teachers and Loved Ones, step back and allow life to be exactly what it is. It may not fit our pictures, but we are in greater harmony with the ultimate health that composes the core of our being. There may be some dreams we've had for this lifetime that are unrealistic, and strategies for fulfillment that are based on false understandings of who we really are, and what is within our reach now.

Remember that imperfect health is not an indictment or past life punishment. It is not a curse from our ancestors. Imperfect health is simply one more amazing opportunity to love ourselves unconditionally. So we ask, "How do I love myself when I am suffering, limited, etc.? How do I love and respect myself, as I am loved and respected by the Divine?"

Optimal energy of health can travel through imperfect instruments, humans with restrictions. Honestly, nothing can interfere or permanently obstruct the passage of the essential, profound perfect health that lives within you. With the assistance of your Masters, Teachers and Loved Ones you'll be able to recalibrate so that who you are is open and available for the sharing of this magnificent spiritual expression.

And so for now, we leave this be. Return your attention to this day and close your Records using the Pathway Prayer Process©.

21

Inspired Manifesting & Your Spiritual Growth

We began this spiritual adventure sparked by an internal prompting for more—more aliveness, more awareness, more appreciation—seeking to amplify the attributes of love as tangible proof of our spiritual growth and development.

While temptation lurks (especially when we are tired and vulnerable)—luring us to entertain supernatural transformations, superstitious activities and comic book superpowers—these are not the heart of spirituality. Many of us have learned the hard way that while we enjoy the glamour of these seductive distractions, they are insufficient support for real people living ordinary lives, with actual challenges. Along the way in our quest for spiritual maturity, we have discarded wishful notions and magical thinking. We have come to recognize and honor the reality of spiritual strength in human beings.

Everything spiritual is rooted in love. When we speak of our spiritual growth, we are referring to the expansion and enrichment of our ability to experience love within ourselves, and to share it with others. We have clarified some of our old expectations about our spiritual development, eliminating the most problematic, such as old ideas suggesting that we are "special" when we are simply "unique," equal but different in our humanity. Another troubling notion is that if/when we attain spiritual awareness we'll be in possession of supernatural powers. Talents such as clairvoyance, clairaudience or clairsentience, have no relation to spiritual development. At the extreme end of that spectrum we have levitation, bi-locating and masterful manipulation of the minds of others. All of which may exist for some people, but not as evidence of spirituality. We may have a heart full of love, aching to extend itself to others, but never gain the ability to see auras or detect invisible vibrations like a measuring device.

We set aside these fantastic, fun ideas for a while so we can direct our attention to the truth of spirituality, spiritual growth and our human journey. The new, empowering question is, "How can I experience and express love today? Within the limitations of my human situation, what avenues are open to me?" You may remember from our earlier examination of Soul's Purposes etched into the Soul's blueprint, that the specific ways we experience and share love are unique to our individual identity. The love is infinite, eternal, immortal and universal. Yet, each individual human being has their own specific relationship to that love. Our intention as we explore this matter of our Soul's Purposes is to identify and recognize the unique individual ways we connect and convey that love through us, and into life.

Everyone has the same access to the infinite, eternal oceans of love. I do not have more than you, and you do not have greater access than me. All human beings have the same opportunity; it is not a privilege saved for a select group.

Additionally, our souls are of equal weight or value, and they are perfect, never needing any adjustments or alterations. All souls are perfect. But, you and I both know there are vast differences spanning the spectrum of human beings. We account for that difference by looking at our awareness. What determines our level of accessibility to the infinite reservoir within is our awareness. This is the realm of our work, and our growth. There is no such thing as "soul growth." Our souls are an ideal size, never in need of fertilizer or cleansing agents. Our challenge is to become aware of the truth of the perfection, the flawlessness of our souls and as we do, we gain incremental access to this eternally alive resource within.

Then how do we determine spiritual growth? This wonderful question has a deceptively simple answer: our spiritual growth is measured by expressions of love. Love, as an infinite property, has unlimited forms of expression. The greater our awareness of the presence of infallible, eternal love within us, the grander our sharing. In our certainty of the reality of perpetual love living within us, we are empowered to give generously, share bravely, and receive graciously. Our motivations to protect ourselves, guard against others, fearfully speculate on what may come to pass, all fade away. We never need to think that we are adding more spiritual light to our reserves, because we already and always have limitless access to spiritual light. Our old idea of sending light to others ceases to be necessary as we recognize that all of the light within us is always in every other person. Instead of engaging in faulty imaginary games of sending light to others, we turn our attention to ourselves and our own erroneous understanding. Taking the opportunity to correct our misunderstanding, we remind ourselves of the highest truth that all the love and light here with me now, is also there with you. We begin to dignify the light and goodness in others, respecting their journey to awareness.

On our quest of Inspired Manifesting, we begin to recognize the power of Akashic Light as it illuminates our way, magnifying the truth of the perpetual presence of light, love and goodness, no matter what contrary evidence suggests. We become seekers and finders of the Light. We become part of the solution for the transformation of awareness of humanity, transcending religions, cultures, nations, races and any other false barriers disguising our oneness. We find that we simply cannot contain the compassion, understanding, patience and appreciation we have for ourselves, and every other human being in creation.

How do we know we are growing spiritually? We give more,

222 - DR. LINDA HOWE

we laugh more, we enjoy more, we delight more, we share more, we accept more, we care more and the list goes on. Everyone has their own unique blend of gifts, talents and abilities on hand for the experience and expression of the profound love within. Our fears diminish, we accept ourselves and others, we criticize less, we encourage and uplift more often. We begin to become the people we know in our hearts we are here to be. Our trepidation about being laughed at, misunderstood and mocked falls away. Our actions become a direct statement of who we are, our values and our truth. Our relationships improve because we no longer hide who we are, and we treat others with the kindness and respect they deserve. Life is on a different footing, and it is good.

Significantly, our awareness is also infinite and everlasting, so it is always growing. Our opportunity is to let it grow, expand, reach as we seek and find love and light everywhere. This ever-expanding awareness is thrilling. Traditional religions refer to this as going from "glory to glory to glory." This is a real life path for those of us awakening to our spiritual awareness at this time. We take a step, love more, give greater and then ... we take another step ... and the process never has to end. It is always and forever in action.

If you want to know if you are growing spiritually, ask your family and friends if they can tell if you love them. Are they certain? Then, you are on track. Are they not very sure? It just means you can return to your inner realm and ask for guidance so you become more aware of the infinite love that is the core of your being. With that awareness, it becomes easier to love more. And that's how we know we're progressing.

On our way to Inspired Manifesting, the next phase of our development is to reflect on the Seven Steps for Spiritual Success in light of our focus. We begin to tease out our present state of growth, our ideals, and the world in which we live. Our Soul's Purposes and Destiny always involve all three elements. Let's map out the path ahead with this in mind and see what is actually likely for us in this incarnation! Fret not! It'll be good.

Awareness. In this area, awareness has three focal points. First is our current level of awareness of our spiritual sensitivity and expression. We want to be kind and honest with ourselves in this matter, as the opposite of either will keep us from progressing. Then, we consider our ideal, our intention for our spiritual growth. Being clear and realistic about what constitutes spiritual growth can guide us to fulfilling possibilities. This is also the time to set aside childish, immature notions of spirituality, and any attendant superpowers we have been secretly hoping to earn. The third component is the world in which we live, important because this is the arena for us to express our highest aspirations, most generous sharing and precious connections with other people. At this point, we are waking up to who we are, how we are and where we are as spiritual beings in human form.

Acceptance. Acceptance does not imply or require approval; it simply requires recognition of the way things are. This is our opportunity to recognize the strengths and weaknesses of our spiritual status, without undue criticism. As humans we are always "works in progress," so our perceived imperfections need never shock nor offend us. They are to be expected. We look again at the aims we have for our spiritual growth, recognizing what is within reach at this point in time and what is beyond us at present. This does not imply failure, but does recognize the progressive, incremental nature of growth, and one step at a time as being the most reliable strategy for our fulfillment. Turning our attention to the world in which we live, we are invited to accept what we find. Not that we are pleased with the way things are going, but we respect the unfolding of life around us as a reality for us to respect. This is particularly difficult when we are in the midst of great social, economic, political, cultural upheaval. We don't have to enthusiastically embrace what we don't like; we simply have to recognize that this is the way things are right now, with or without our personal consent. This vital step is required if we want to grow and be effective in our world.

Appreciation. Now comes the Herculean task of finding positive value for ourselves at every level, our spiritual growth, our ideal and the world. Until we do, and it must be sincere, we won't be able to move ahead or make a decisive difference in any of this. Perhaps the greatest challenge is appreciating the positive value of our stuckness, our limited spiritual awareness and any confusion impeding us. Remember, we only but always embrace ideas because they are our highest option at any given time. No person ever has decided to hurt themselves or others just for sport. If and when that occurs, the selection has been made because the harmful selection seems to be the best choice, the one that will bring about more love, than any other. With this in mind, take a fearless look and find the ways in which you can honestly appreciate yourself, your journey and the world.

Appropriate Action. As always, action is involved, even with our spiritual growth. We can begin to identify all activity as spiritual activity, but not every action is personally productive. All action on earth is an opportunity to expand our conscious connection with Ultimate Reality. But, not every action benefits every individual. Our challenge is to experiment and learn what actions we can take in our life, right now, to enrich our sense of the infinite love living within. And then, do it! Moving in that direction, we naturally relinquish those activities that stir up unpleasant feelings, and generate undesirable consequences. Pay attention. Your personal happiness is a reliable indicator of what actions are appropriate or not for you.

Assessment. We continue to observe and evaluate ourselves and our experiments. What are we doing that ignites our awareness of the infinite love within? What are we doing that is taking us away from that perception? These are not standardized answers. What works very well for me, could make you miserable, and vice-versa. Observe, evaluate and make new choices. It's a great privilege for us humans to be able to discern and select. Let's use this gift to propel ourselves in our preferred directions.

Adjustment. Now that we have some good information about ourselves and our unfolding, we can make some changes. What a privilege it is to do this! Go ahead and make the adjustments that make good sense to you. Your common sense is your ally in this process. This is the time to fine tune your habits, practices, rituals and everyday activities to bring you closer to the experience of the infinite within. Sometimes we have dramatic changes to make and, other times, slight tweaks. As living human beings on an eternal quest, we are always in this process. As we live and learn, we apply our new insights to ourselves for the purpose of empowering our awareness and living more consciously in the light of life.

Allow and Enjoy! Our work is almost complete. Now we are asked to step back and allow life, the goodness, the light of life to take over for us. We have made our way into the heart of light and here we encounter the powerful pulse of life that is always available to carry us to our next level of fulfillment. And it's enjoyable. Our personal happiness is a requirement for our spiritual growth. It's evidence that we are in an expanding awareness of the Ultimate Reality mined through our human experience.

Exercise: Seven Steps to Spiritual Success

Now, let's go into our Akashic Records to explore these seven steps and let the Akashic Light illuminate more to support our transformation. Open your Records using the Pathway Prayer Process©.

In the sacred sanctuary of your own Akashic Records, settle in, opening your awareness to the Akashic atmosphere, which is characterized by a unique blend of loving attributes, customized for you at this point in time. Take a minute to identify and name the specific qualities you encounter in this space. While you are getting comfortable, open up to the presence of your dedicated spiritual advisors: your Masters, Teachers and Loved Ones. You'll never see them with your human eyes, or even your strong spiritual eyes, but you'll be able to detect their presence by the traits of love and support directed to you.

Now, let's begin this exploration with the first step, Awareness. Bring to mind your current understandings of your own spiritual condition, your ideals and the life you're living. Ask your Masters, Teachers and Loved Ones to shine the Akashic Light on this entire matter so that you can more easily sense the highest truth and greatest possibility for yourself at this time. Continue to hold the Light steady as it penetrates through your present reality into a deeper layer of insight and wisdom. The surface elements remain the same, but it's as if you can get a sense of the underpinning or the spiritual context for all of it. It is common to have a startling moment of awareness. Your current awareness is ideal for delivering you to this time. Your ideals have been invigorating, and your comprehension of your life have been supported by your awareness. But that it is like the tip of the iceberg, there is more for you—so much more.

Life holds nothing against you, but cherishes you for your valiant efforts to grow. With this Awareness, we go to step 2, Acceptance. In the grace-infused space of your Records, it is easier than usual to accept yourself for where you are, the way you understand, your clarity and confusion. Accepting life just the way it is becomes infinitely more possible within our Records. The loving Light of the Akasha shines perpetual compassion, patience and understanding on all humans, at all times. Here is our chance to begin to perceive as if we are divine in nature, only registering the highest potential and greatest attributes of all persons. Acceptance implies that we allow life to be just the way it is, as we allow the same to all other people and especially to ourselves. Here is our opportunity to accept ourselves as we are accepted in divine consciousness.

Appreciation follows Acceptance. Typically, we stumble over criticism and judgements of ourselves, others and the world at this point. It seems like too great a stretch to appreciate the positive value of our limitations and the foibles of others, but that is our challenge. This is true spiritual reaching. How do I love and appreciate myself when I have been so fearful, clinging to my old ideas, hard on people I love and dismissive of those I don't know? How do I love myself even though I have been so confused and seemingly derailed on the spiritual path? How do I love myself even though I've been anxious about fulfilling my destiny?

Superstitious? And so judgmental about the world and its

ways? Yes, this is a pivotal step in our spiritual growth, to be able to know and love ourselves and others unconditionally, as we are known and loved by the Divine.

Ask your Masters, Teachers and Loved Ones to empower you to take this transformational step on your journey. With their support from behind, companionship alongside and leading with the Akashic Light, your success and satisfaction are assured. You can do this, and you will. This is the lifetime you've long awaited for just this opportunity. Now is the time. It's your time.

With a measure of Appreciation, we move to Appropriate Action. Asking our Masters, Teachers and Loved Ones to shine the pure and powerful Akashic Light on some options for us, inspiring us to take appropriate action. To be more specific, we want to determine what actions will accelerate our spiritual growth at this time in our lives. And if we've been considering some activities that cause us some uncertainty, we ask for clarity. What can we do to ignite our spiritual awareness, to hasten our development, to be inspired to seek more ways to experience and express love? Our Masters, Teachers and Loved Ones are at the ready, but will not impose ideas on us. We are expected to use our minds, involve our hearts and engage our will, through actions. Our next step makes it safe to experiment, it's Assessment. Go ahead and make a selection and do it. No harm will come to you.

Having gathered some useful information, we are invited to Assessment. In the loving company of your Masters, Teachers and Loved Ones, observe and evaluate your actions to decide what is helpful, and what is not beneficial. The important question here is this, "Does my action bring me a stronger sense of love or a dimmer sense of love?" We are seeking activities that stimulate the unlimited treasury of love within, and avoiding actions that encourage other qualities. The Akashic point of view is valuable here because of its kindness and respect. In this Akashic atmosphere, it is safer for us to be honest with ourselves, to see and know more clearly without fear of ridicule. Emotional safety is one of the great benefits of spiritual exploration in the Akashic Field. You are wise to take advantage of this realm.

Our Assessments made, we continue to make our Adjustments. As infinite beings involved in an eternal quest, we have come to understand that change is a natural part of our journey. Recognition and willingness to make adjustments is evidence of a strong sense of being known and loved in a wise and compassionate universe. Shine the Akashic Light on what you determine to be in need of adjustment. What needs to change? Review in this Light. Reflect on the actions you must take to fulfill this adjustment. Ask for the strength and the courage to be the person who makes adjustments with ease and grace. It will be given to you. Make the adjustments so your future actions bring you closer to your spiritual ideal of total conscious contact with the Ultimate Reality. This is your birthright. And now is your time.

Allow and Enjoy! Stepping back and allowing yourself to be exactly who you are, the way you are at this point in time is a spiritual gift beyond all measure.

Allowing life to be just what it is, without condemnation or irritation, is a spiritual treasure. Allowing yourself to experience the process of conscious spiritual growth is generous beyond belief. With this shower of remarkable spiritual gifts, you are absolutely entitled to enjoy yourself and your life, as is. Perceived imperfections are not a blockage, just look past them. Life loves you and enjoys you as you awaken. We do not have to achieve perfection or full enlightenment to be known and loved by life. Life is the journey. Your happiness is evidence of your spiritual growth. Be happy. And so for now, we leave this be and together we close our Records.

ONWARD!

When I first started writing this book, I believed we were in the most unusual times. On every continent we were facing failing economies, distorted political systems, faltering religions, crumbling social structures, and the collapse of every possible organization and structure. Today, I look back wistfully on those times, and chuckle at my own naiveté.

What's different? COVID-19, novel coronavirus—a global pandemic that is sweeping through our world—is changing everything. We are in the midst of a health terror upending human life as we know it in the 21st century, bringing the last vestiges of the old order to a certain demise. This virus exposes all the fault lines in our structures and institutions, along with the erroneous assumptions serving as foundations. The problems are glaring, and solutions seem slippery. Democratic in nature, the virus attacks all social, racial, economic, political, age and familial groups. No one is exempt. Globally, governments are scrambling to keep their citizenry out of harm's way, with varied success.

What is the spiritual issue at play here? Precisely, a planetary problem revealing this fundamental spiritual truth: We are all one. In this crisis, the only way we have any hope of resolving this mess is by recognizing the reality of our unity, our oneness. Although this has been true since the beginning of time, just brought to our attention now, we can get a clear awareness of the reality of our existence. We are all one. Everyone on Earth is connected, interrelated, whether we like it or not. Reality is what it is, with or without our express approval. We have returned to that simple but profound spiritual principle of acceptance.

The challenge at hand is this. Until and unless we accept the reality of our oneness, we are doomed to chronic and urgent, even deadly, repetitions of this virus. Only by accepting and embracing the truth of our unity will we be able to resolve this challenge of challenges and move ahead to peaceful times.

Many people have been asking me, "How can I stop this COVID-19 using the Akashic Records?" The answer is, "You cannot." That is not the point. By relying on the infinite light and love of life, each one of us will be sufficiently inspired and empowered to be the generous, loving people we are meant to be. We can no longer wait for life to improve, it may never happen. But, we need not wait.

Now is the time. We do not have to be perfect in our efforts to help. Life asks only that we be sincere in our sharing, kind to ourselves and others, and open minded, willing to act on solutions as they become evident. Life is perfect, the light is perfect. No need to worry or to wait for our personal idea of perfection to be realized.

Our spiritual awareness is a gift to help us navigate times just as ridiculous and unfathomable as the one we are in. It is not here so we can get into a wrestling match with others, to show off our spiritual prowess, to manipulate the virus or any of the people who are annoying us with their incompetence. Our spiritual awareness is a gift of inner peace and clarity about the goodness of life and the essential loving nature of all humans. Even as we see our political leaders act like rogue teenage boys, we know they are doing what they believe to be the best. And, at some level, they represent what we believe as well, or they would not be in power. Here, we can ask, "How can I love myself when the political leaders are idiots—and selfish ones at that!?"

The truth of spiritual awareness is not that it is a weapon we can use to change circumstances. Rather, it is a state of consciousness providing us with a grace, that spiritual fairy dust, not to make matters worse, but to find ways to experience and express love in the middle of madness. What a wonderful gift!

No matter what is happening around us, no matter what horrific experiences we endure, we always have a choice. Our choice is to look for ways to experience and express love, right here and now. Given the situation, what action can I take that stimulates the infinite love within, and encourages me to share it with others?

This is the opportunity we have been waiting for! You and I are here by divine appointment, to be a part of the great transformation of human consciousness. This virus is our ally in this change. Our opportunity is to know the truth of who we are, and who every other person is as well. We are here to fearlessly seek and find light and goodness in others, at a time when it's easy to lose sight of that inner eternal flame.

With the altitude of Akashic awareness, we have the possibility to rise above these hair raising situations—illness, poverty, confusion, strife and all the relations of fear. We are the ones who can live in the world by not being bogged down by it, because we know the truth. We recognize the absence of malice in everyone and appreciate their efforts even when (and sometimes especially when) we disagree.

Our clear awareness of our unity makes it possible for us to be gracious and respectful even when our planetary traveling companions have values different from our own. We realize that no one can extinguish the light of our Soul, diminish our ability to love or interrupt our capacity to enjoy moments of Heaven on earth. These are treasures of the Soul we have been cultivating for lifetimes and, with the Akashic Records using the Pathway Prayer Process©, we open the chest of riches for our own fulfillment and the upliftment of others.

What does *Inspired Manifesting* mean in these times? It means that we have an open channel between our minds, hearts, wills and souls. The blueprint of our Soul, our destiny, is embedded within us—to be experienced and expressed through us as the people we are at this point in time. Your Soul's Purposes are important particular ways for you to activate the infinite, eternal well of love that is the core of your being. These are the pathways to allow that love to flow through you, out into the world. They make us happy, to recognize and act on these fundamental truths of who we are.

If you need money to bring your Soul's Purposes to life, you will be able to get it. If you don't need money, you won't have it. Money and material acquisition is not the point. The point is this: How do I ignite the eternal flow of love within me so that I experience it in my everyday life and share it with others? Keep experimenting. Do your part. Don't worry about others, everyone is on their own path, and all paths are valuable. Enjoy yourself and those you encounter. These are the best of times.

What inspires you will bless the world. And the whole world is waiting.

Join me. Don't be concerned about your human imperfections. Life doesn't hold that against you! This is not a passive lifetime! It is not about perfection or imperfection. It is about discovering your unique usefulness, and participating to the best of your ability. The perfect light and love of life uses only imperfect persons.

Join us. Trust that, as we make our way in the world in the best way we know how, the light will lead us, guide us and accompany us. We are never alone. We are all together now, reaching out our hands to one another ... together, we are indeed the light of the world.

I'll be looking for you! And when we meet in person, remind me of our amazing Akashic journey and the wonders we discovered together. We'll never have another lifetime like this, so let's enjoy every moment.

Much love and many blessings,
Linda

THANK YOU!

Thank you: simple, precise and true. The best way I have to express the explosion of gratitude in my heart for all the people who have extended themselves and their talents to me throughout this journey.

Of course, I begin with my Lisa. Support, appreciation, understanding...you know when to encourage me to go beyond my fears and when to let go. I love you. Michael, thanks for laughing at my jokes and living your life on your own terms.

To my beloved "A" team: Jean Lachowicz, Susan M. Lucci, Brian Fischer, Rev. Cindy Waldon, Mark James, Ravyn Guy and Rachel Zargo. You fill my days with hope, light and love. And to Patty Collinsworth, Alyson Mead, Juliet Kibbe and The Foxhole folks—thank you for your generosity.

My gratitude continues for Kathleen Martin, Sharon Black, Rev. Melissa Blevins, Anne & Amy, Diana and Liz, Natasha, Andrew and the boys, Carina and Theo, Steffany Barton, Dr. Dawn Silver, Shelia Leidy, Bobbi Vogel, Cathy Geen, David Pond, Marc St. Camille, Kevin Theis and Paul Stroili.

Students can access my teachings online thanks to Sidney Slover's team at Learn it Live. My work now reaches the ends of the Earth thanks to Mark Deng and his team in China, Rosemary and Simon Chao and the team in Taiwan, including Austin Chen.

I love you all. Together we are doing what we could never do alone.

ABOUT THE AUTHOR

 **Dr. Linda Howe** is the leading expert specializing in using the Akashic Records—the energetic archive of souls—for personal empowerment and transformation. By making her Pathway Prayer Process© freely available to all, she became the first person to bring conscious, reliable access to the Records to the worldwide community.

A teacher in the field for more than two decades, Dr. Howe founded the Center for Akashic Studies in 2001. Her inspired, comprehensive curriculum has been revealed to her through her relationship with the Akasha and refined through her work with thousands of students over the years. Through in-person and online classes, award-winning books, and social media, she shares optimal ways to tap into the timeless wisdom of the soul for practical application in the uncertainties of daily living.

Linda Howe's publications have been translated into many languages and include: the ground-breaking, award-winning essential book *How to Read the Akashic Records*, *Healing through the Akashic Records* and *Discover Your Soul's Path through the Akashic Records*.

Dr. Howe is the first person ever to earn a Doctorate in Spiritual Studies with a specialty in the Akashic Records, from Emerson Theological Institute.

You are invited to sign up for classes, purchase books and learn more about her at her website: www.LindaHowe.com. Reach Dr. Howe for speaking engagements and more at linda@lindahowe.com.

CPSIA information can be obtained
at www.ICGtesting.com
Printed in the USA
BVHW040902200121
598218BV00015B/466